Maritime Tankers: Terrorist Threats, Consequences and Protective Measures

MARITIME TANKERS: TERRORIST THREATS, CONSEQUENCES AND PROTECTIVE MEASURES

THOMAS P. NAYLOR

EDITOR

Nova Science Publishers, Inc.
New York

Copyright © 2009 by Nova Science Publishers, Inc.

All rights reserved. No part of this book may be reproduced, stored in a retrieval system or transmitted in any form or by any means: electronic, electrostatic, magnetic, tape, mechanical photocopying, recording or otherwise without the written permission of the Publisher.

For permission to use material from this book please contact us:
Telephone 631-231-7269; Fax 631-231-8175
Web Site: http://www.novapublishers.com

NOTICE TO THE READER
The Publisher has taken reasonable care in the preparation of this book, but makes no expressed or implied warranty of any kind and assumes no responsibility for any errors or omissions. No liability is assumed for incidental or consequential damages in connection with or arising out of information contained in this book. The Publisher shall not be liable for any special, consequential, or exemplary damages resulting, in whole or in part, from the readers' use of, or reliance upon, this material.

Independent verification should be sought for any data, advice or recommendations contained in this book. In addition, no responsibility is assumed by the publisher for any injury and/or damage to persons or property arising from any methods, products, instructions, ideas or otherwise contained in this publication.

This publication is designed to provide accurate and authoritative information with regard to the subject matter covered herein. It is sold with the clear understanding that the Publisher is not engaged in rendering legal or any other professional services. If legal or any other expert assistance is required, the services of a competent person should be sought. FROM A DECLARATION OF PARTICIPANTS JOINTLY ADOPTED BY A COMMITTEE OF THE AMERICAN BAR ASSOCIATION AND A COMMITTEE OF PUBLISHERS.

LIBRARY OF CONGRESS CATALOGING-IN-PUBLICATION DATA

Available Upon Request

ISBN: 978-1-60692-205-7

Published by Nova Science Publishers, Inc. ✛ *New York*

CONTENTS

Preface		vii
Abbreviations		1
Chapter 1	Results in Brief	7
Chapter 2	Background	13
Chapter 3	Energy Commodity Shipments Face Varied Threats, and a Successful Attack Could Have Substantial Consequences	25
Chapter 4	Although Stakeholders Are Taking Protective Measures, Implementation Challenges Pose Difficulty Both Abroad and at Home	39
Chapter 5	Stakeholders Have Developed Spill and Terrorism Response Plans but Face Several Challenges in Integrating Them	55
Chapter 6	Conclusions	75
Chapter 7	Recommendations for Executive Action	79
Chapter 8	Agency Comments	81
Appendix I: Objective, Scope, and Methodology		85
Appendix II: Selected Energy Commodities Transported by Tanker into United States		89

Appendix III: Recent High-Profile Terrorism Incidents
　　　　　　　　against Tankers and Energy Infrastructure　　　**91**

Appendix IV: Assessing and Managing Risks
　　　　　　　　Using a Risk Management Approach　　　　　　**93**

References　　　　　　　　　　　　　　　　　　　　　　　　**97**

Index　　　　　　　　　　　　　　　　　　　　　　　　　　**107**

PREFACE

U. S. energy needs rest heavily on ship-based imports. Tankers bring 55 percent of the nation's crude oil supply, as well as liquefied gases and refined products like jet fuel. This supply chain is potentially vulnerable in many places here and abroad, as borne out by several successful overseas attacks on ships and facilities. This book addresses (1) the types of threats to tankers and the potential consequences of a successful attack, (2) measures taken to protect tankers and challenges federal agencies face in making these actions effective, and (3) plans in place for responding to a successful attack and potential challenges stakeholders face in responding. The review spans several foreign and domestic ports, and multiple steps to analyze data and gather opinions from agencies and stakeholders.

This is an excerpted and edited version of a GAO Report.

In: Maritime Tankers
Editor: Thomas P. Naylor

ISBN: 978-1-60692-205-7
© 2009 Nova Science Publishers, Inc.

ABBREVIATIONS

ACP	Area Contingency Plan
AMSC	Area Maritime Security Committee
AMSP	Area Maritime Security Plan
BLEVE	boiling liquid expanding vapor explosion
CBP	Customs and Border Protection
CDC	certain dangerous cargo
COTP	Captain of the Port
CSF	Critical Skill Factor
DHS	Department of Homeland Security
DOD	Department of Defense
DOJ	Department of Justice
EPA	Environmental Protection Agency
FBI	Federal Bureau of Investigation
ICS	incident command system
IMO	International Maritime Organization
ISPS	International Ship and Port Facility Code
LNG	liquefied natural gas
LOOP	Louisiana Offshore Oil Port
LPG	liquefied petroleum gas
MARSEC	Maritime Security Condition System
MIRP	Maritime Incident Recovery Plan
MLA	Maritime Liaison Agent
MOTR	Marine Operational Threat Response Plan
MTR	Maritime Transportation Response
MTSA	Maritime Transportation Security Act of 2002

NCP	National Oil and Hazardous Substances Pollution Contingency Plan
NIMS	National Incident Management System
NRP	National Response Plan
NSFCC	National Strike Force Coordination Center
ONS	Operation Neptune Shield
OPA 90	Oil Pollution Act of 1990
SAFE Port Act	Security and Accountability for Every Port Act of 2006
SONS	Spill of National Signficance
USCG	United States Coast Guard

December 10, 2007
The Honorable
John D. Dingell Chairman

The Honorable
Joe Barton
Ranking Member Committee on Energy and
Commerce House of Representatives

The Honorable
Bennie G. Thompson
Chairman

The Honorable
Peter King
Ranking Member Committee on Homeland Security
House of Representatives

The Honorable
Edward J. Markey
House of Representatives

This is a public version of a report we issued in March 2007 that contained Sensitive Security Information related to the transportation of energy commodities by tanker. Specific details regarding the nature of security conditions and operations at specific ports, and specific findings related to response plans and results of exercises that are sensitive were removed. We worked with the cognizant agencies to ensure that this version would not contain Sensitive Security Information. No additional audit work was performed for the completion of this version. The conclusions and recommendations of our March 2007 report remain generally unchanged.

The United States economy is dependent on oil, gas, and other energy commodities that are transported from overseas by ship.[1] For example, in 2005, approximately 55 percent of the nation's crude oil supply—one of the main sources of gasoline, diesel and jet fuel, heating oil, and many other petroleum products—and approximately 3 percent of the natural gas supply, was imported by tanker. Daily ship-based imports of crude oil averaged about 8.5 million barrels, or the equivalent of about four supertankers arriving at U.S. terminals each day.[2] In addition to crude oil, the United States also imports highly combustible liquid energy products, such as gasoline, jet fuel, and liquefied gases, such as liquefied petroleum gas (LPG) and liquefied natural gas (LNG).[3] Natural gas is converted to LNG by cooling it to minus 260 degrees Fahrenheit, at which point it becomes a liquid. In its liquid form, natural gas reduces to more than 1/600th of its volume as a gas, making it feasible to transport over long distances. Daily ship-based imports of LNG now average about 1.7 billion cubic feet, or the equivalent of two LNG tankers arriving at a U.S. port every 3 days. This already extensive reliance on imported energy commodities is expected to increase—and for LNG, to grow substantially. The Energy Information Administration forecasts that by 2015, the amount of crude oil imported into the United States will increase by nearly 4 percent, while the amount of imported LNG will grow more than 400 percent.

Transporting these often hazardous commodities by sea involves a global supply chain with many players. For energy commodities imported by the United States, this supply chain has three main activities: loading it aboard a ship at a foreign facility, shipping it across oceans and waterways, and unloading it at a facility in this country. Waterborne shipments originate at facilities in a variety of countries—for crude oil, primarily in Mexico, Saudi Arabia, Venezuela, and Nigeria, and for LNG, primarily in Algeria and Trinidad and Tobago.[4] Overseas facilities where tankers are loaded are owned by the private sector, governments, or combinations of the two. Foreign governments play a substantial role in overseeing the security of energy export operations. Shipment of these commodities likewise involves vessels owned by many different companies, as well as transportation routes across international waters that no government controls. In 2006, there were approximately 3,550 registered crude oil tankers of 300 gross tons or more, along with 200 registered LNG tankers. Most of these vessels are registered in countries other than the United States, which means the

United States has limited oversight authority over these vessels' crews or condition until they enter U.S. waters. Once the crude oil or LNG tanker arrives in the United States, it is unloaded at terminals that may be on the Atlantic, Gulf, or Pacific coasts. LNG is currently unloaded at one of five locations.[5] As demand for natural gas grows, the number of domestic LNG unloading locations is expected to increase. The Federal Energy Regulatory Commission, which must approve each onshore LNG terminal siting and construction application, has already approved 11 additional terminals, and dozens more have been proposed.[6]

This supply chain, while critical, is also vulnerable to disruption by terrorists. Port facilities are inherently vulnerable, because they must provide access by land and sea and because they are sprawling installations, often close to population centers. Likewise, the ships that transport these products are vulnerable because they travel on direct routes that are known in advance and, for part of their journey, they may have to travel through waters that do not allow them to maneuver away from possible attacks. Since so many different players are involved, terrorists have room to probe the supply chain for the weakest link. Despite an often heavy security presence, terrorists have attempted—and in some cases carried out—several attacks on this supply chain since September 11, 2001. To date, these attacks have included attempts to damage tankers or disrupt loading operations in or near overseas ports. For example, in 2004 terrorists coordinated an attack against two offshore oil terminals in Iraq where tankers were loading, and in 2002 terrorists conducted a suicide boat attack against the French supertanker *Limburg* off the coast of Yemen.

Much of the international framework for protecting this supply chain and preventing pollution from vessels is laid out in international conventions. The International Ship and Port Facility Security (ISPS) Code was adopted under the auspices of the International Maritime Organization (IMO) by the Conference of Contracting Governments to the International Convention for the Safety of Life at Sea (SOLAS).[7] In accordance with the SOLAS Convention as amended in 2002, the code establishes requirements for contracting governments of countries where ports are located, contracting governments of countries where ships are registered, operators of port facilities, and operators of vessels traveling on the high seas.[8] Individual nations can set higher standards for facilities on their soil and for vessels registered in that country. The United States has chosen to set higher standards, largely through the Maritime Transportation Security Act of 2002 (MTSA).[9] Enacted after the September 11, 2001, attacks, MTSA places much of the responsibility for coordinating and overseeing security efforts with the federal government—and more specifically with the Department of Homeland

Security (DHS) and its agencies, such as the U.S. Coast Guard. Another international agreement developed under IMO auspices is the International Convention for the Prevention of Pollution from Ships, which entered into force in 1983 and was intended to prevent pollution of the marine environment by ships from operational or accidental causes. Included in its provisions was pollution by oil, chemicals, and harmful substances. In the United States, Congress passed the Oil Pollution Act of 1990 (OPA 90) following the 1989 *Exxon Valdez* oil spill.[10] OPA 90 addressed prevention, response, and compensation for oil pollution from vessels and facilities in U.S. waters and the shoreline. OPA 90 greatly increased federal oversight of maritime oil transportation by setting new requirements for vessel construction and crew licensing and manning, mandating contingency planning, enhancing federal response capability, broadening enforcement authority, and increasing penalties.[11]

In setting U.S. policy with regard to homeland security, both Congress and the Administration have endorsed making decisions on the basis of risk—that is, on identifying critical infrastructure, determining what is most at risk, and applying sound measures designed to make cost-effective use of resources and funding. As groups such as the 9/11 Commission have pointed out, no amount of money can totally insulate seaports from attack by a well-funded and determined enemy. Managing on the basis of risk acknowledges the trade-offs inherent in deciding how finite resources should be spent.

Federal actions to prevent attacks against the energy supply chain involve coordination with the many players involved, including foreign governments; foreign and domestic corporations that own and operate the ships that carry energy commodities; companies that import, refine, and market petroleum and liquefied gases; and a host of state and local governmental agencies. At the state and local levels, fire and police departments would be the first responders, with support from emergency management, environmental, and transportation departments. Private sector agencies, such as oil or gas facility terminal operators, vessel management companies, and oil spill response organizations, would also be involved. Finally, multiple federal agencies would also respond. In particular, the U.S. Coast Guard (USCG) and the Federal Bureau of Investigation (FBI) would have primary responsibility for leading the response effort.

To help evaluate how secure the maritime energy supply chain is and how the United States would respond in the event of a terrorist attack, you asked us to review security and safety efforts taken to date.[12] This report addresses three questions:

What are the types of terrorist threats to tankers carrying energy commodities and the potential consequences of a successful attack?

What measures are being taken to protect these tankers, and what challenges do federal agencies face in making these actions effective?

If a terrorist attack succeeds despite these protective measures, what plans are in place to respond and what are the potential challenges in responding to an attack?

To address these objectives, we conducted a wide range of activities overseas and in the United States. Overseas, we met with officials from the IMO, foreign government security agencies, vessel and facility operators, international industry associations, vessel and cargo insurers, and risk management companies. We conducted our overseas work primarily in five countries, which we selected for specific reasons related to their role in the supply chain, the sophistication of their security procedures, or the presence of key stakeholders. In the United States, we met with officials in many federal departments and agencies, including the Departments of Homeland Security, Defense, State, Energy, Transportation, and Justice; the Federal Energy Regulatory Commission; and the Environmental Protection Agency. We met with a variety of state and local government officials dealing with homeland security, emergency response, and law enforcement, as well as with operators of oil cleanup organizations, petroleum tankers, liquefied gas carriers, and their attendant unloading facilities. We also visited field units of the U.S. Coast Guard, Customs and Border Protection, the FBI, and a nonprobability sample of petroleum and liquefied gas import and export facilities.[13] In these visits we observed security practices firsthand, and conducted interviews with officials. We obtained and reviewed studies on the consequences of an attack, obtained additional views from experts, and specifically convened a panel of academic and industry experts to determine the potential consequences of an incident involving LNG.[14] We analyzed databases, progress reports, regulations, and guidance documents we obtained from the Coast Guard and Federal Energy Regulatory Administration. We obtained necessary information from the Coast Guard to review the reliability of the information contained in the databases used in this report. Appendix I contains a more detailed discussion of our methodology. We conducted our work in accordance with generally accepted government auditing standards from April 2005 through February 2007.

In: Maritime Tankers...
Editor: Thomas P. Naylor

ISBN: 978-1-60692-205-7
© 2009 Nova Science Publishers, Inc.

Chapter 1

RESULTS IN BRIEF[*]

Attacks overseas show that tankers face several major types of threats that, if carried out domestically, could have serious consequences. Overseas, terrorists have demonstrated the ability to carry out at least three main types of threats. First—and overall of greatest concern to officials we spoke with—is a suicide attack, such as the 2002 suicide boat attack on the tanker *Limburg* off the coast of Yemen. This attack killed 1 person, injured 17, and spilled 90,000 barrels of oil. A second major type of threat, known as a "standoff attack," uses a rocket or other weapon launched at a sufficient distance to allow the attackers to evade defensive fire. A third type of threat is an armed assault. For example, well-armed bands have used small boats to attack tankers, loading facilities, and oil workers. Many other types of potential attacks exist, such as internal crew conspiracies and collisions with other vessels piloted by terrorists. To date, no such attacks have occurred on tankers in U.S. waters or on loading facilities in U.S. ports, and intelligence officials report there is currently no specific credible threat to tankers or terminals on the domestic front. Nonetheless, these successful attacks abroad, the expressed desire by terrorists to target U.S. economic interests, and the potential outcome of a terrorist attack on a tanker have led Congress and the Administration to conclude that protective efforts are warranted. A successful attack on an energy commodity tanker could have substantial public safety, environmental, and economic consequences. Public safety and environmental consequences of an attack vary by commodity. For instance, highly combustible commodities like LNG and LPG have the potential to catch fire, or in a more unlikely scenario—if they are trapped in a confined space such as under a dock—

---

[*] Excerpted from GAO Report GAO-08-141, dated December 2007.

explode, posing a threat to public safety. Crude oil and heavy petroleum products remain in the environment after they are spilled and must be removed, potentially causing significant environmental damage. Finally, the economic consequences of a major attack could include a temporary price spike reflecting fears of further attacks, and supply disruptions associated with delays of shipments if major transit routes, key facilities, or key ports are closed. The loss of one cargo of an energy commodity might not have a significant, sustained price impact. However, if an attack results in port closures for multiple days or weeks, price responses and higher costs could mean losses in economic welfare to consumers, businesses, and government amounting to billions of dollars.

Much is being done, both internationally and domestically, to protect energy commodity tankers and their attendant facilities from attack, but notwithstanding these actions, significant challenges may still leave tankers and facilities at risk. Internationally, many foreign governments and facility operators are taking such actions as improving physical security at facilities and conducting offshore patrols. For example, port facilities report compliance with ISPS Code requirements, tanker operators report strengthening their security posture while loading and at sea, and the Coast Guard visits foreign exporting ports to assess the effectiveness of the anti-terrorism measures in place. Navies of various countries, including the United States, are also patrolling threatened waters, such as the Persian Gulf and the Gulf of Aden, due to attacks on ships, including tankers, and port facilities. International stakeholders face challenges, however, in implementing this security framework. Our visits to overseas facilities showed that some port facilities had put extensive security measures in place, while at other facilities, we found such problems as unattended gates and downed fences. Although facilities may report they are complying with the ISPS Code, there is no mechanism currently in place to verify compliance, and Coast Guard activities abroad are limited by and dependent on conditions set by host nations, including the locations the Coast Guard can visit. For tankers in transit in international waters, the primary challenge involves patrolling the lengthy travel routes and frequent danger spots with a limited number of naval vessels. Because of the challenges and limitations faced internationally, security efforts taken domestically carry increased importance. Here, federal agencies such as the Coast Guard and Customs and Border Protection (CBP) have taken a variety of steps to protect the energy supply chain. Both agencies monitor arriving ships and crews, and the Coast Guard also conducts security activities, such as pre-entry security boardings, escorts, and patrols. The prioritization of the Coast Guard's security activities is based upon its established risk-based decision-making processes. These activities are often reinforced by local law enforcement units that, in some cases, receive financial support from facility operators. Despite these domestic efforts, challenges persist. Coast Guard records document that at some ports, a lack of resources has hindered some Coast Guard units from meeting their self-imposed requirements for security activities, such as escorts and boardings. To better align security requirements with its resources, the Coast Guard recently revised some of its security standards, such as those for protecting vessels carrying a number of hazardous liquids and liquefied gases. Although the Coast Guard reported that it based this action on the consequences of an attack, it could not provide us any analyses that covered all commodities involved. As a result, it is unclear if security requirements were reduced for the commodities with the lowest associated risk. The Coast Guard is currently performing such an analysis. In the future, the Coast Guard faces additional challenges at some domestic ports, where workload demands are likely to rise substantially as new LNG facilities come on line and LNG shipments increase. These increased demands could cause the Coast Guard to continue to be unable to meet the standards it has set for keeping U.S. ports secure.

Should a terrorist attack succeed despite the protective measures in place, the United States and designated ports have developed plans for responding but could face several challenges in implementing these plans effectively. Specifically, ports face challenges in integrating both national- and port-level spill and terrorism response plans, mitigating economic consequences, and obtaining necessary resources to respond. Regarding the plans, at the national level, the National Response Plan lays out the broad parameters of the federal role, both in spill response (that is, taking steps to contain a spill and mitigate its environmental damage, regardless of how it occurred) and in terrorism response (that is, for the attack, taking security-related actions and conducting an investigation). The plan designates the Coast Guard as the primary agency for spill response on water and the FBI as the primary agency for terrorism response, and it calls on the two agencies to coordinate their responses if the incident involves an attack on energy commodity tankers. Other federal plans and agreements also come into play, each with information about coordinating responses among the various agencies involved or taking specific action. At the port level, under the Oil Pollution Act of 1990 and the Maritime Transportation Security Act of 2002, Coast Guard's Captain of the Port is to establish separate plans for spill and terrorism responses, working with local agencies, which are subsequently approved by Coast Guard districts. For both types of response plans, the agencies may include port authorities, fire departments, and facilities in the port. Some stakeholders, such as private oil spill response organizations, participate only in spill response planning, while other stakeholders, such as police departments, participate mainly in terrorism response planning. While national- and port-level plans exist, federal agencies and ports could face challenges in using them effectively.[15] First, the separate spill and terrorism response plans should be integrated for responding to an attack on an energy commodities tanker. At the federal level, the Coast Guard and the FBI should ensure that they have a detailed operational plan to integrate the spill and terrorism response sections of the National Response Plan. Port stakeholders should integrate spill and terrorism response plans to address response coordination. The Coast Guard has recommended joint exercises when feasible to test stakeholders' spill and terrorism response plans. Second, the President's strategy for maritime security recommends that ports develop plans to mitigate the economic consequences of an attack, such as determining priorities for allowing vessels to enter or leave the port after it reopens. While such plans could be developed under the leadership of the Coast Guard's Captain of the Port at the port level, there was no national-level guidance about what economic mitigation plans should contain at the time of our review. Finally, some ports we visited may not have the resources needed to promptly respond to an attack. For instance, some local firefighters said that they may not be able to effectively respond to marine fires because they do not have enough fire boats or are not sufficiently trained for shipboard firefighting. Port officials also said they lacked resources for improving emergency response capabilities. According to DHS officials, federal grant funding for response activities may become more available as DHS moves toward a more comprehensive risk-based process for allocating grant funds. However, DHS may not be able to effectively allocate grants on the basis of reducing risk because it does not have performance measures showing how much of a given resource is needed to conduct a response. Without such performance measures, the federal government cannot effectively set priorities for acquiring needed response resources.

We are making recommendations to the Secretary of Homeland Security and the Attorney General designed to build on efforts already under way and make these efforts more effective. For protecting against threats, we recommend developing a national resource allocation plan for meeting security requirements posed by proposed expansion in the number of LNG facilities and shipments. For responding to actual attacks, these recommendations include ensuring that a detailed operational plan has been developed that integrates the different spill and terrorism response sections of the National Response Plan, as well as ensuring the integration of local spill and terrorism planning and exercises at ports that receive energy commodities; developing national-level guidance that ports can use for mitigating economic consequences, particularly in the case of port closures; and developing specific performance measures for determining the resources needed to effectively respond to attacks on tankers carrying energy commodities. The responsible agencies generally agreed with our recommendations. DHS, however, stated it was taking the final recommendation (on performance measures) under advisement.

Chapter 2

BACKGROUND

MANY STAKEHOLDERS ARE INVOLVED IN SECURING THE MARITIME ENERGY SUPPLY CHAIN

Numerous international and domestic organizations play a role in the security of maritime energy commodities. The list of stakeholders outside the United States is quite diverse. They include international organizations, governments of nations where tankers load or where tankers are registered, and owners and operators of tankers or facilities (see table 1).

On the domestic side, the U.S. Coast Guard is the lead federal agency and is responsible for a wide array of maritime safety and security activities. Other U.S. government agencies support the Coast Guard's maritime security mission by addressing a wide range of issues that affect the flow of cargo and people into the United States. State and local governments and the private sector also have responsibilities to secure domestic ports. Table 2 lists key federal agencies and other stakeholders on the domestic side, together with examples of the kinds of maritime security activities performed.

Table 1. Selected International Stakeholders with Maritime Security Activities

Agency Internatrional Organizations	Selected mission-related activities
• International Maritime Organization (IMO) IMO is an organization responsible for regulating international shipping with 167 governments as members.	• Develops and maintains a comprehensive regulatory framework for shipping. • Develops international standards for port and vessel security.
• International Maritime Bureau • The International Maritime Bureau is a division of the International Chamber of Commerce that works to suppresspiracy around the world.	• The International Maritime Bureau's Piracy Reporting Center broadcasts a daily bulletin of piracy attacks directly to ships at sea. • Provides piracy updates and comprehensive reports on a regular basis. • Reports piracy incidents to law enforcement authorities.
• Intertanko Intertanko is an association of independent tanker owners and operators.	• Intertanko maintains a database that includes reports of security conditions at ports of call throughout the world.
• BIMCO The Baltic and International Maritime Council (BIMCO) represents over 65 percent of world's tanker fleet.	• BIMCO coordinates with international organizations, governments, and members to improve port and ship security, address piracy and stowaway problems, secure an adequate supply of well-trained seafarers.
Overseas governmental agencies	
• ISPS designated authorities Government agencies responsible for implementing ISPS requirements. In the United States the authority is the United States Coast Guard.	• Set security levels at a country's ports. • Review vessel and facility security plans and oversees compliance with these plans.
International private sector	
• Overseas port facility operators	• Implement facility security plans that meet local port security standards.
• Vessel owners and operators	• Implement vessel security plans that meet ISPS Code and flag state security standards.
• Lloyd's Market Association Support and research organization for Lloyd's insurance underwriters.	• Lists area endangered by war, strikes, terrorism, and related perils—areas for which underwriters can charge higher premiums for vessels.

Source: GAO.

Table 2. Selected Domestic Stakeholders with Maritime Security Activities

Stakeholders	Selected mission-related activities
Federal government: Department of Homeland Security	
• U.S. Coast Guard	• Conducts vessel escorts, boardings of selected vessels, and security patrols of key port areas. • Ensures vessels in U.S. waters comply with domestic (MTSA) and international (ISPS Code) maritime security standards. • Reviews U.S. vessel and facility security plans and oversees compliance with these plans. • Meets with foreign governments and visits foreign port facilities to observe security conditions.
• Customs and Border Protection (CBP)	• Screens vessel, crew, passenger, and cargo information prior to vessel arrival in the United States. • Boards all vessels that arrive from foreign ports to review personnel and cargo documentation. Ensures that all have appropriate documents to gain access to the United States. • If concerns about crew or cargo exist, takes action to deny entrance to the United States.
Federal government: Department of Justice	
• Federal Bureau of Investigation (FBI)	• FBI Maritime Liaison Agents, stationed at key ports in the United States, help disseminate maritime intelligence to port stakeholders. • Leads Joint Terrorism Task Forces. • Has lead role in investigating maritime terrorism incidents.
Federal government: Department of Defense	
• U.S. Navy	• Provides support to Department of Homeland Security as requested for maritime homeland security operations. • Maintains a credible maritime interdiction capability to deal with identified hostile ships at any location when authorized to do so. • Builds relationships with partner nations' navies to enhance cooperation and information sharing.
Federal government: Department of State	
• Bureau of Consular Affairs – Visa Services	• Reviews visa applications and issues nonimmigrant visas for crew members, including recognizing falsified documents on visa applications.
State and local governments	
• Law enforcement agencies	• Conduct land-based patrols of port facilities. • If agency operates a marine unit, support Coast Guard role through water patrols and possibly escorts.
Private sector	
• Facility operators	• Develop and implement facility security plans that meet MTSA standards.

Source: GAO.

All of these international and domestic stakeholders help to ensure the safety and security of a global supply chain that brings energy commodities to the United States. This supply chain spans the globe and reaches many regions of the world. Each day, the United States imports many different energy commodities from overseas suppliers in Africa, Europe, the Middle East, and North and South America. Excluding Canada, which supplies petroleum and natural gas to the United States via pipeline, the vast majority of these varied imports arrive by tanker.

TANKERS TRANSPORT ENERGY COMMODITIES AROUND THE WORLD

The various types of energy commodities require different handling methods, and as a result, various kinds of tankers have been built to accommodate them. An LNG carrier is designed for transporting LNG at minus 260 degrees Fahrenheit, when gas liquefies and shrinks drastically in volume. The cargo is transported in special tanks insulated to minimize evaporation. LNG carriers are up to 1,000 feet long and have a draft (depth below the water line) of 40 feet when fully loaded. The global LNG fleet is expected to double from 200 in 2006 to over 400 by 2010. According to industry reports, the existing fleet has completed more than 33,000 voyages without a substantial spill. Oil tankers are more numerous and vary greatly in size. Tankers transporting crude oil from the Middle East generally consist of Very Large Crude Carriers, which typically carry more than 2 million barrels of oil per voyage.[16] These ships are over 1,000 feet long, nearly 200 feet wide, and have a draft of over 65 feet.[17] Figure 1 shows a typical Very Large Crude Carrier. These ships are too big for most U.S. ports and must transfer their loads to smaller tankers (a process called lightering) or unload at an offshore terminal. At present, the United States has only one such offshore terminal—the Louisiana Offshore Oil Port (LOOP).[18] Most tankers transporting cargos from the Caribbean and South America, by contrast, are smaller than Very Large Crude Carriers and can enter U.S. ports directly.

There are generally two enforcement systems aimed at ensuring that these vessels are in compliance with applicable regulations, laws, and conventions: flag vessel is registered. Flag state control can extend anywhere in the world where the state control and port state control. The flag state is the country in which the vessel operates. For example, a flag state's requirements set the standards for the operation and maintenance of all vessels flying that flag. If the flag state is a

Source: U.S. Navy.

Figure 1. Oil Tanker at Al-Basrah Offshore Oil Terminal, Persian Gulf.

contracting government to the SOLAS Convention, these standards are required to be at least as stringent as those included in the ISPS Code. The port state is the country where the port is located. Port state control is the process by which a nation exercises its authority over foreign-flagged vessels operating in waters subject to its jurisdiction. It is intended to ensure that vessels comply with all domestic requirements for ensuring safety of the port, environment, and personnel. Thus, when a foreign-flagged oil tanker enters a U.S. port, the U.S. port state control program, administered by the U.S. Coast Guard, becomes the primary means of marine safety enforcement. For example, the Oil Pollution Act of 1990 requires that all tankers built after 1994 coming to the United States must have double hulls—that is, a two-layered hull to help prevent spills resulting from a collision or grounding (see figure 2).[19]

According to the Energy Information Administration, the United States consumes more than 20 million barrels of petroleum every day.[20] Of that amount, over 65 percent comes from foreign sources.

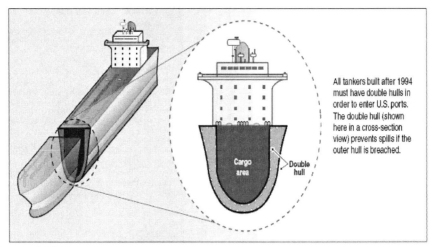

Source: GAO.

Figure 2. Tanker with Insert of Double Hull.

ENERGY COMMODITIES ORIGINATE IN A VARIETY OF LOCATIONS

The top suppliers of crude oil and petroleum products to the United States in 2005 were Canada, Mexico, Saudi Arabia, Venezuela, and Nigeria—each supplying over 1 million barrels of petroleum per day (see figure 3). Iraq, Algeria, Angola, Russia, and the United Kingdom are also major energy suppliers with daily imports to the United States of up to 500,000 barrels per day. These top 10 energy suppliers accounted for approximately 75 percent of all U.S. petroleum imports in 2005. All petroleum imports to the United States from those countries arrive on tankers, except those from Canada.

Imports are a growing portion of the natural gas supply in the United States. With consumption of natural gas growing faster than domestic production, imports of natural gas will almost certainly continue to rise, according to the Energy Information Administration. Today, Canada is the primary supplier of natural gas to the United States and all of natural gas imports from Canada are carried by pipeline.[21] Approximately 3 percent of all natural gas imports to the United States is LNG. Trinidad and Tobago is the single largest supplier of LNG to the United States, supplying 70 percent of all LNG imported into this country (see figure 4). Other LNG suppliers in 2005 included Algeria, Egypt, Malaysia, Nigeria, Qatar, and Oman.

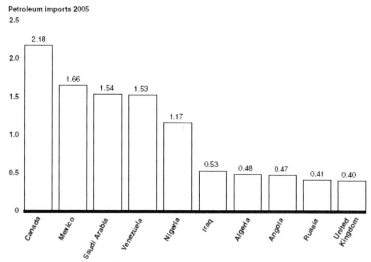

Source: Energy Information Administration.

Figure 3. Top Exporters of Petroleum to the United States in 2005 (Millions of barrels per day).

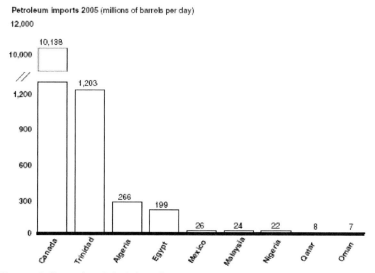

Source: Energy Information Administration.

Figure 4. Top Exporters of Natural Gas to United States in 2005 (Millions of cubic feet per day).

KEY DOMESTIC PORTS HANDLE VAST MAJORITY OF ENERGY IMPORTS

The United States imports about 65 percent of its crude oil and petroleum products as well as about 3 percent of its natural gas needs.[22] As shown in figure 5, certain energy commodities are imported into particular regions of the country. Appendix II provides detailed descriptions of U.S. energy commodity imports transported by tanker. For example, in 2004:

Ports along the Gulf Coast imported 62 percent of the crude oil imported to the United States.
Ports along the East Coast imported 95 percent of the gasoline and 75 percent of the LNG.
Ports along the West Coast imported 60 percent of all jet fuel.

Source: GAO analysis of Energy Information Administration data.

Figure 5. Regional Significance of Petroleum Commodities.

The global maritime environment through which the energy supply chain operates is constrained by physical geography and influenced by regional political dynamics. The physical geography of the continents, for example, forces shipping lanes to pass through certain narrow channels, or chokepoints. There are approximately 200 such locations, but only a handful are of strategic importance for the global energy supply (see figure 6). A chokepoint by definition tends to be shallow and narrow, resulting in impaired navigation and congestion from other tankers, cargo ships, and other smaller vessels, which can impede the free and efficient flow of goods. Moreover, several key chokepoints are surrounded by more than one sovereign nation, resulting in a complex security environment within a constrained physical space. Managing security in this environment requires significant coordination among these countries to successfully manage the security in these locations. According to the Energy Information Administration, chokepoints are susceptible to pirate attacks and shipping accidents in their narrow channels. In addition, chokepoints can be blocked, mined, or rendered inaccessible by foreign naval forces, with potentially devastating consequences for the flow of oil and goods around the world and into the United States.

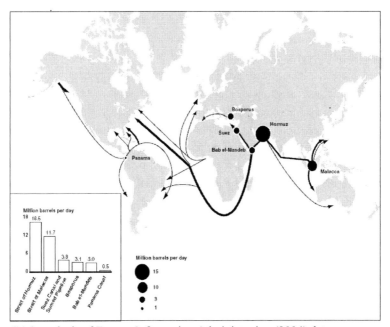

Source: GAO analysis of Energy Information Administration (2004) data.

Figure 6. Oil Flows and Strategic Shipping Chokepoints.

The Straits of Hormuz and Malacca are two critical maritime shipping chokepoints that tankers pass through regularly. The Strait of Hormuz, which connects the oil fields of the Persian Gulf with the Gulf of Oman and the Indian

Ocean, is the most important chokepoint in the world in terms of the global energy supply, with about 20 percent of the world oil supply, including 17 percent of U.S. petroleum imports passing through it. Tankers with oil from the Persian Gulf must navigate through this chokepoint in order to access the principal international shipping lanes toward the United States. Another chokepoint, the Strait of Malacca, links the Andaman Sea and the Indian Ocean (and oil coming from the Middle East) with the South China Sea and the Pacific Ocean (and major consuming markets in Asia). The Strait of Malacca is located among Malaysia, Indonesia, and Singapore and about 600 vessels pass through it each day. Piracy and political instability in the region, especially in Indonesia, are issues of concern for shipping operations in the strait. The Energy Information Administration identified other important maritime chokepoints, including the Bab el-Mandab passage from the Arabian Sea, the Panama Canal connecting the Pacific and Atlantic Oceans, the Suez Canal connecting the Red Sea to the Mediterranean Sea, and the Bosporus Straits linking the Black Sea to the Mediterranean Sea.

Besides facing vulnerabilities while in transit, vessels can be vulnerable while moored at facilities where they are receiving or unloading their cargoes, and the energy-related infrastructure located in ports can also be vulnerable to attack. Vessels transiting into and out of ports and their attendant infrastructure can be vulnerable in a number of ways. During transit into and out of port, these vessels travel slowly, which increases their exposure. Tankers follow timetables that are easy to track in advance and they follow a fixed set of maritime routes. Once tankers arrive in this country, they must wait offshore for pilots to navigate the ship channels into many of the nation's ports.

Since the terrorist attacks of September 11, increased national attention has been focused on the potential vulnerability of the nation's 361 major seaports to terrorist attack. According to the *National Strategy for Maritime Security*, the infrastructure and systems that span the maritime domain have increasingly become both targets of and potential conveyances for dangerous and illicit activities.[23] GAO has previously reported that ports are vulnerable because they are sprawling, interwoven with complex transportation networks, close to crowded metropolitan areas, and easily accessible.[24] Ports and their maritime approaches, including waterways and coastal areas, facilitate freedom of movement and the flow of goods while allowing people, cargo, and vessels to transit with relative anonymity. Some energy terminals are located in open seas where they are accessible by water or air, while others are located in metropolitan areas, along key shipping channels, or near pristine environmental sanctuaries where they may be accessible by water, air, or land.

ADDRESSING TANKER SECURITY VULNERABILITIES INVOLVES SETTING RISKS IN THE CONTEXT OF OTHER SECURITY AND NONSECURITY PRIORITIES

In the wake of the terrorist attacks of September 11, 2001, there was widespread acknowledgement that numerous and substantial gaps existed in homeland security. There is also widespread acknowledgment, however, that resources for closing these gaps are limited and must compete with other national priorities. It is improbable that any security framework can successfully anticipate and thwart every type of potential terrorist threat that highly motivated, well-skilled, and adequately funded terrorist groups could perpetrate. While security efforts clearly matter, various groups like the 9/11 Commission have emphasized that total security cannot be bought no matter how much is spent on it. In short, the nation cannot afford to protect everything against all threats, even within the relatively narrow context of tanker security. Choices are clearly involved—including decisions about the relative vulnerability posed by attacks on energy commodity tankers as compared with attacks in other forms, such as air safety or security in crowded urban centers.

In this context, risk management has become a widely endorsed strategy for helping policymakers make decisions about allocating finite resources in such circumstances.[25] It emphasizes the importance of assigning available resources to address the greatest risks, along with selecting those strategies that make the most efficient and effective use of resources. Risk management has received widespread support from Congress, the President, and the Secretary of Homeland Security as a tool that can help set priorities and inform decisions about mitigating risks.[26]

In: Maritime Tankers...
Editor: Thomas P. Naylor

ISBN: 978-1-60692-205-7
© 2009 Nova Science Publishers, Inc.

Chapter 3

ENERGY COMMODITY SHIPMENTS FACE VARIED THREATS, AND A SUCCESSFUL ATTACK COULD HAVE SUBSTANTIAL CONSEQUENCES

Even though intelligence sources have reported that there are currently no specific credible threats to energy tankers in U.S. waters or their attendant facilities on U.S. soil, attacks overseas show that tankers face several major types of threats, and if a threat were to be successfully carried out domestically, it could have serious consequences. Overseas, terrorists have demonstrated the ability to carry out at least three types of threats.[27] First, and of greatest concern, according to officials we spoke with, is a suicide attack against a tanker or attendant facility. Second is a standoff missile attack using a rocket or some other weapon launched from a distance. Third is an armed assault by terrorists or armed bands while a tanker is moored or in transit. There are additional types of threats, including internal crew conspiracies and collisions with a vessel piloted by terrorists. While attacks have so far occurred only overseas, two Coast Guard admirals testified before Congress that malicious maritime incursions into U.S. waters, such as immigrant or drug smuggling, occur regularly. If an attack on a commodity tanker were successful in U.S. waters or while docked at a U.S. unloading facility, substantial public safety, environmental, and economic consequences could result. Public safety and environmental consequences of an attack vary by commodity. For instance, LNG and LPG are highly combustible and pose a risk to public safety of fire or—in a more unlikely scenario in which they are in a confined space—explosion. The environmental impact, however, of LNG and LPG spills would be minimal since they dissipate in a short period of time. Crude oil and heavy petroleum products remain in the environment after they are spilled and must be removed, potentially causing significant environmental damage. Potential economic consequences of an attack include psychological market responses as well as significant delays and possible shortages if major transit routes, key facilities, or ports are closed.

NO CREDIBLE SPECIFIC THREAT OF ATTACK AT U.S. PORTS TO DATE, BUT EVENTS OVERSEAS INDICATE REASONS FOR CONCERN

According to U.S. government intelligence sources, there have been no specific credible terrorist threats to tankers in U.S. waters or their unloading facilities on U.S. soil in the wake of the September 11 attacks. Nonetheless, several events overseas and intelligence reports indicate ongoing concern about the potential for an attack against tankers or energy facilities.

Heightened security threat levels in response to potential threats. The Coast Guard has raised the Maritime Security (MARSEC) level from Level 1 to Level 2 on several occasions in response to nonspecific threats based on intelligence or other warnings to the maritime sector.[28] In the past, the Coast Guard has raised the MARSEC level due to general threats.

Other intelligence indicating ports are targets under consideration. Security officials in the U.S. government are concerned about the possibility of a terrorist attack in a U.S. port in the future. For example, captured terrorist training manuals cite seaports as targets and instruct trainees to use covert means to obtain surveillance information for use in attack planning. Terrorist leaders have also stated their intent to attack infrastructure targets within the United States, including seaports, in an effort to cause physical and economic damage, and inflict mass casualties.

Continued policy priority for port security. Four years after passage of the Maritime Transportation Security Act of 2002, Congress remained sufficiently concerned about maritime security to again increase security efforts under the Security and Accountability Act for Every (SAFE) Port Act of 2006.[29] This law (1) required the Department of Homeland Security to conduct terrorist watch list checks of newly hired port employees, (2) provided authority for risk-based funding through security grants to harden U.S. ports against terrorist attacks and enhance capabilities to respond to attacks and resume operations, and (3) required the Department of Homeland

Security to develop protocols for resuming trade after a transportation security incident.

Officials Are Concerned about Three Primary Types of Threats

Our discussions with officials of various agencies and our review of reports and other published documentation indicate that the following three types of attacks on tankers or attendant facilities are considered to be the most likely.

Suicide Attacks

In the maritime domain, suicide attacks have been carried out using a small, explosive-laden boat or vehicle that the attacker rams into a tanker or energy facility. The intent of such an attack is maximum damage to human or physical targets without concern for the life of the attacker. Previous attack history underscores terrorist intentions and capability to use small boat attacks. Moreover, intelligence experts say that the suicide boat attack uses a proven, simple strategy that has caused significant loss of life and significant damage to commercial and military vessels.

Several suicide attacks have been carried out against tankers and energy infrastructure in the Persian Gulf region. They have taken place in restricted waterways where a ship's ability to maneuver or engage the attackers is hampered or when a ship has stopped or moored. For example:

> In April 2004 terrorists attacked the Al-Basrah and Khawr Al'Amaya offshore oil terminals in Iraq using vessels packed with explosives. Several oil tankers were either docked at or in the vicinity of the offshore terminals during the attack. Even though the speedboats detonated prematurely and missed striking the oil tankers and the offshore terminals, another small craft near the Khawr Al'Amaya terminal exploded when coalition forces attempted to intercept it, killing two U.S. Navy sailors and a U.S. Coast Guardsman. According to a recent study on maritime terrorism, the coordinated attack appears to have been part of an overall terrorist strategy to destabilize Iraq, and both terminals were shut down for 2 days, resulting in lost revenue of nearly $40 million.[30]
>
> Another suicide attack occurred in October 2002 when terrorists rammed the French supertanker *Limburg* as it slowed for a pilot to approach the Ash Shihr

Terminal off the coast of Yemen. (See figure 7.) The resulting explosion breached the *Limburg*'s double hull and ignited stored oil on board the vessel. An estimated 90,000 barrels of oil were spilled, 1 crewman was killed, and 17 were injured.

In addition to maritime suicide attacks, terrorists have also targeted energy facilities on land. In February 2006, for example, terrorists attempted to drive vehicles packed with explosives through the gates of a major oil-processing facility in Saudi Arabia's eastern province. Al Qaeda claimed responsibility for the attack, which killed two Saudi guards and represented the first direct assault on a Saudi oil production facility.

Source: AFP.

Figure 7. Tanker *Limburg* after Terrorist Attack near Yemen.

Standoff Attacks

A second type of threat against tankers and attendant maritime infrastructure is a standoff missile attack using a rocket, mortar, or rocket-propelled grenade launched from a sufficient distance to evade defensive fire. Standoff missile attacks have been aimed at military ships in ports in the Persian Gulf, but these kinds of attacks also represent a serious type of threat against tankers. Terrorists launched such an attack using Katyusha rockets in 2005, narrowly missing two U.S. naval ships moored at a Jordanian port.

Compared to suicide attacks, standoff attacks are easier to execute, but are less likely to be as effective, according to intelligence experts. The range, size, and accuracy of explosive projectiles used in such an attack could vary considerably.

Armed Assaults

Armed assaults, particularly at critical shipping chokepoints, represent a third major type of threat to tankers along the energy supply chain, according to the International Maritime Bureau. These attacks on tankers and energy infrastructure have taken place where maritime security is lacking and they have been carried out in most cases by pirates seeking to gain control of the ship for financial gain, including petty theft and kidnapping of crew for ransom.[31] Pirate attacks against tankers and cargo ships have taken place in numerous locations, including off the coast of Somalia, in the Gulf of Guinea and Persian Gulf, and along the Strait of Malacca. According to officials at the International Maritime Bureau, oil tankers account for about one-quarter of all pirate attacks. Pirate groups armed with automatic weapons have seized tankers in the Strait of Malacca and off the coast of Somalia.

For example, in March 2006 pirates armed with automatic weapons hijacked a tanker off the coast of Somalia and demanded ransom payments for the release of the ship and its crew. Also, attacks on offshore oil facilities have become commonplace in Nigeria, where local rebel groups claim to be fighting the Nigerian government over control of oil revenue. While no attacks on international oil tankers off the coast of Nigeria have occurred to date, militant groups in the area have threatened to escalate the conflict by attacking ships.

Other Types of Threats Are Considered Less Likely

There are other types of threats besides the three above, but assessments we reviewed and officials we met with indicated these other scenarios were less likely to occur. Two examples cited were the following:

Crew conspiracies. Coast Guard intelligence reports suggest a hypothetical possibility that crew members (or persons posing as crew members) could conspire to commandeer a tanker with the intent of using the vessel as a weapon or disrupting maritime commerce. Vessel operators and industry groups do not consider this to be a serious threat, especially given the technical complexity of modern gas carriers and large oil tankers and the extensive vetting process for crew on these kinds of vessels. Crew conspiracy could also result in situations where oil tankers or gas carriers could be used to transport terrorists. Intelligence officials estimate that the number of overall stowaways on all vessels entering U.S. ports was expected to average 30 per month in 2005. There have been cases of stowaways with suspected terrorist connections on board U.S.-bound vessels since 2000.

Collisions. One scenario related to armed assaults involves pirates or terrorists hijacking a large ship and ramming it into a tanker, an energy facility, or critical infrastructure such as a bridge. Although such scenarios require gaining control of a ship, terrorists' successful takeover of aircraft in the September 11 attacks demonstrate that such plans could be feasible. To date, there have been no known cases of terrorists intentionally using a vessel as a weapon, but there have been some close calls in pirate-prone areas. Security experts point to an example in 2003 in which a group of pirates gained control of the chemical tanker *Dewi Madrim* in the Strait of Malacca. Once at the tanker's helm, the pirates altered the ship's speed, disabled communications, and steered the ship for over 1 hour before escaping with equipment and technical documents.

Intelligence Reviews Indicate Threats Are Likely to Persist

Reports we reviewed and assessments we received indicate that the threat of seaborne terrorist attack on maritime energy tankers and infrastructure is likely to persist. The information we reviewed and discussions we had with agency officials indicate the greatest degree of concern remains overseas. For example, in October 2006 it was reported that there were threats against Saudi Arabia's Ras

Tanura oil terminal, which is the world's biggest offshore oil facility, as well as a refinery in Bahrain. As part of its mission in the area, the U.S. Navy, together with coalition forces, continues to patrol areas containing critical maritime energy infrastructure to ensure their security, and works with regional navies in the Persian Gulf to improve their ability to enforce maritime security. In addition, Coast Guard maritime threat assessments we reviewed consider the threat of terrorists attacking vessels outside U.S. territorial waters to be significant. According to these reports, future maritime terrorist attacks are most likely to occur in the Persian Gulf, Red Sea, Mediterranean Sea, and Southeast Asia.

Domestically, intelligence reports and other assessments continue to disclose incidents that demonstrate the need for continued concern about potential terrorist threats. For example, two Coast Guard admirals testified that the nation is subject to an estimated four malicious maritime incursions around the country each week.[32] These incursions represent opportunities to infiltrate homeland security and could cause widespread human, economic, and environmental damage in our nation's maritime points of entry. Most of these incursions to date have involved vessels bringing illegal immigrants, drugs, or other contraband into the country.

POSSIBLE CONSEQUENCES OF AN ATTACK INCLUDE PUBLIC SAFETY, ENVIRONMENTAL, AND ECONOMIC IMPACTS

A successful attack on an energy commodity tanker could have substantial public safety, environmental, and economic consequences. Public safety and environmental consequences vary by commodity. LNG and LPG are highly combustible and pose a risk to public safety of fire and explosions, but their environmental impact would be minimal since they dissipate in a short period of time. Crude oil and heavy petroleum products do not dissipate quickly and must be removed from the water, posing a greater environmental than public safety risk. Economic consequences of an attack could be substantial, not so much because of the loss of a tanker or its cargo, but because of the greater shock to the economy, particularly if major transit routes, key facilities, or ports are closed. Price spikes that reflect fears or expectations about the price and supply of energy commodities could also be significant.

PUBLIC SAFETY AND ENVIRONMENTAL CONSEQUENCES VARY BY COMMODITY

LNG and LPG spills pose primarily a public safety hazard to structures and people because of the potential for fires and explosions. These gaseous energy commodities are transported as liquids either by cooling or by pressurizing the gas. If spilled, they will return to their gaseous state, causing vapor to form above the spill. It is these vapors that will burn. Further, the vapors will drift away from the site of the spill if not immediately ignited by a source such as an open flame or strong static charge. Once ignited, the fire will travel back through the vapors toward the initial spill site and, if fuel remains, continue to burn near the tanker.

One of the key elements of how a fire will affect the public is the amount of heat that is radiated away from the fire. The amount of heat radiated away from a fire is related to how smoky the fire burns—fires with a great deal of smoke radiate much less heat because the dark smoke absorbs the radiation. LNG and LPG vapor fires burn very cleanly, with little smoke, and thus emit more heat than light petroleum product or crude oil fires.

Besides the danger of fire, there is also a danger of explosions if LNG or LPG vapors are ignited in a confined area, such as under a dock. If the attack on a tanker occurred in a congested port area, an explosion could damage infrastructure or harm people located nearby. In addition to potential explosions of confined vapors, a particular type of explosion—called a boiling-liquid-expanding-vapor explosion—can occur on tankers that carry pressurized cargoes, such as some LPG tankers.[33] In these tankers, the individual tanks carrying the LPG may rupture violently if they are compromised by heat or explosion. Since LNG is not transported in pressurized tanks, then this type of an explosion is not likely to occur.

Finally, people who come in contact with spilled refrigerated liquefied gases could be burned due to the cryogenic (freeze) nature of the liquid. LNG and LPG are both transported internationally in refrigerated tankers that keep the gas so cold that it retains a liquid form. A spill of either LNG or LPG could expose people close to the spill to the cold liquid and cause cryogenic burns or frostbite. This is not likely to affect the public, but could affect the crew on the tanker or other people located close to the tanker.

LNG and LPG spills pose little threat to the environment because they almost entirely vaporize in a matter of minutes or hours and disperse into the atmosphere. If an LNG or LPG spill were ignited, there could be localized impacts on wildlife near the fire, but few other environmental effects.

Spills of light petroleum products, such as gasoline, diesel, and jet fuel, can have both public safety and environmental consequences. Light petroleum products produce flammable vapors when they are spilled. These vapors can be ignited and could result in large, damaging fires. Further, the vapors could drift away from the site of the spill if not immediately ignited by a source such as an open flame or strong static charge. Once ignited, the fire will travel back through the vapors toward the initial spill site and, if fuel remains, continue to burn near the tanker. Besides the danger of fire, there is also a danger of explosions if light petroleum product vapors are ignited in a confined area, such as under a dock. If the attack on a tanker occurred in a congested port area, an explosion could damage infrastructure or harm people located nearby.

Spills of light petroleum products have varying environmental impacts, depending on conditions. Light petroleum products evaporate—almost all of the spill can evaporate in a few hours or up to a day. Consequently, light petroleum products generally do not persist in the environment for long unless the spill is churned by significant wave action. In that case, such products can mix with water and will linger in the environment for much longer periods of time. A 1996 spill highlighted the damage that can occur when a light distillate oil is spilled in heavy wave conditions, resulting in much of the oil mixing with water rather than evaporating. In this case, a tank barge carrying home heating oil was grounded in the middle of a storm near Point Judith, Rhode Island, spilling approximately 20,000 barrels of heating oil. An estimated 80 percent of the release was mixed into the water, with only about 12 percent evaporating and about 10 percent staying on the surface of the water.[34] The spill affected animals and plants living on the sea bed, with an estimated mortality of 9 million lobsters, 19.4 million clams, 7.6 million rock and hermit crabs, and 4.2 million fish. The oil spill resulted in a fishing closure for about 250 square miles in Block Island Sound for a period of 5 months.

Spills of crude oil and heavy petroleum products could result in significant environmental consequences. Since these types of spills do not readily evaporate, they can linger in the environment. Environmental cleanup of crude oil and heavy petroleum product spills can take several years and in some cases cost billions of dollars. According to ExxonMobil, the company spent $2.2 billion on the *Exxon Valdez* cleanup. Crude oil and heavy petroleum products can mix with water, particularly in the presence of waves, causing small drops of water to be trapped inside the spilled oil. This is called an emulsion and can hamper cleanup by making the spilled oil difficult to skim off the water. This will greatly increase the volume of the spill, since the water trapped within the oil also has to be removed. In addition, residual oils are sometimes more dense than water, allowing them to sink and contaminate bottom sediments. Finally, crude oil and heavy petroleum products can coat birds and marine mammals, both smothering the organisms and exposing them to them to hypothermia as their feathers and fur lose the ability to insulate.

While crude oil and heavy petroleum products evaporate, they produce few flammable vapors. For instance, less than half of a crude oil spill and 10 percent of heavy petroleum product spills will evaporate into vapors that could burn or explode. While fire always raises concerns about public safety, the smaller volume of vapors available to burn would result in small fires that are less likely to endanger the public.

BLOCKAGE OF KEY TRANSIT ROUTES, KEY FACILITIES, OR PORTS COULD COST BILLIONS

Although the *Exxon Valdez* accident demonstrates that even one spill can create substantial environmental cost, an attack that affects only a single tanker is unlikely to have significant consequences on the overall economy, other than a relative short-term market price increase. One tanker carries a small percentage of the total daily demand for a commodity. As mentioned above, Very Large Crude Carriers typically carry more than 2 million barrels of oil per voyage, which is about 10 percent of U.S. daily oil consumption. In most cases, the relatively small volume in an individual tanker could be replaced with other imports or from domestic storage. Two examples show the relatively small effect on supply if the broader supply network is not substantially affected:

> The approximately 240,000 barrels of oil released into Prince William Sound by the *Exxon Valdez* represented about 20 minutes of total U.S. oil consumption in 1989. The spill's actual disruption was somewhat greater: According to the Department of Energy, the incident actually resulted in an oil supply disruption of 13 million barrels of oil over 13 days, because the spill restricted tanker transport in Prince William Sound and the volume of oil piped from the Alaskan North Slope also had to be reduced. Still, even this 13 million barrel disruption represented only about 18 hours of total national consumption.[35]
>
> More recently, an approximately 6,300-barrel oil spill in November 2004 significantly reduced tanker traffic on a stretch of the Delaware River for more than a week. As a result, a nearby refinery had to reduce production of

refined products because of reduced crude oil availability. The oil spill also threatened to contaminate the water intake system of a nuclear power plant along the river, which was temporarily shut down. Despite these reductions in energy supply, gasoline prices actually dropped in the days after the oil spill.

The loss of a tanker carrying crude oil or heavy petroleum commodities will pose additional economic costs for ship replacement and environmental cleanup. Tankers can cost about $150 million, and the lost cargo could cost over $100 million dollars more. The Delaware River oil spill cleanup cost about $175 million over the course of 1 year. As the $2.2 billion *Exxon Valdez* spill cleanup illustrates, a larger spill or a spill in a more sensitive ecological zone could cost much more.

A much more significant impact could occur if an attack on a tanker resulted in the closure of a port, damage to a key facility, or long interruption of a key transit route. A successful attack while a tanker was docked, for example, could result in damage to a key facility. Even if a port were not closed altogether, the Coast Guard could increase the MARSEC level at one or more ports or industries to MARSEC 3—the highest level. The Coast Guard noted in the *Federal Register* that MARSEC Level 3 will involve significant restriction of maritime operations that could result in the temporary closure of individual facilities, ports, and waterways, in either a region or the entire nation. Depending on the nature of the specific threat, this highest level of maritime security may have a considerable impact on the stakeholders in the affected ports or maritime areas. The ability to estimate the costs to business and government for even a short period at MARSEC Level 3 is difficult to do with any level of accuracy or analytical confidence due to the infinite range of threats and scenarios that could trigger MARSEC Level 3. The Coast Guard also noted that the length and the duration of the increased security level to MARSEC Level 3 will be entirely dependent on the scope of transportation security incidents or disasters that have already occurred. The Coast Guard expects MARSEC Level 3 to increase the direct costs to businesses attributable to increased personnel or modified operations, and it also expects indirect costs to society of the "ripple effects" associated with sustained port closures would greatly outweigh the direct costs to individual businesses.

The scale of these effects can perhaps be seen in several hypothetical examples, both international and domestic.

Strait of Hormuz. Each day, tankers transport 20 percent of global daily oil consumption—about 17 million barrels of oil—through the Strait of Hormuz, the narrow waterway that connects the Persian Gulf with the Arabian Sea.

While there are some limited alternatives for exporting oil from the Persian Gulf without going through the strait, these alternatives could not make entirely for the amount of oil lost by closure of the strait. While the United States and other oil-importing countries have reserves of crude oil that they could use to mitigate the loss of supply from the Persian Gulf, oil could not be withdrawn fast enough to entirely make up the lost volumes. For example, while the U.S. Strategic Petroleum Reserve has 688 million barrels of oil, the send-out capacity of the reserves is only 4.4 million barrels per day. Other countries face similar constraints. Additionally, if closure of Hormuz lasted for an extended period of time, strategic reserves could run out or become so low as to be unable to mitigate any additional petroleum supply disruptions.

Northeast United States. An attack on a key port in the northeastern United States, such as Boston, could result in energy commodity shortages or price spikes. For instance, the LNG facility near Boston (in Everett, Massachusetts), is the only facility importing liquefied natural gas in the Northeast. LNG is very important to the Northeast during heating season because natural gas movement into the Northeast is constrained during the winter because existing pipelines to New England are fully utilized. A report prepared by the Power Planning Committee of the New England Governor's Conference, Inc., concluded that if LNG from the Everett facility and satellite operations elsewhere in the region is not available on a peak winter day, the region could have insufficient gas supply to meet the needs of all customers for space heating and some key electric generators. An attack that damages the Everett LNG facility during a cold winter could result in natural gas shortages or price spikes.

LOOP. A loss of import capacity at the LOOP could increase the price of crude oil and refined products. LOOP is a key energy facility—a terminal in the Gulf of Mexico that, according to DOE, accounts for more than 10 percent of total U.S. crude oil imports. LOOP and its storage terminals are connected to more than 50 percent of the refining capacity in the United States. LOOP is also the only facility in the United States that can receive tankers of the ultra-large and very large types. Counteracting the impact of losing LOOP could involve release of oil from the U.S. Strategic Petroleum Reserve and lightering in other U.S. ports.[36]

While we did not find any studies on the economic consequences of closures to energy facilities at ports, other broader reviews of port closures identified possible loses in the billions of dollars. One study of the 2002 West Coast port shutdown, a 11-day closure of all West Coast ports due to a labor dispute, developed estimates (based on models) for the costs of the shutdown based on the losses in income by U.S. workers, consumers, and producers based on trade flow, ability to ship goods, and the inclination of consumers and industries to substitute for other, available goods.[37] The study found that for a shutdown lasting 4 weeks (which was longer than the actual 11-day shutdown) total loses to the U.S. economy would be about $4.7 billion, with industrial consumers bearing the majority of that burden.[38]

Other studies have attempted to model the economic impact of terrorist attacks on ports. For example, one study examined the potential effects of a 15-day port closure at Los Angeles-Long Beach due to a radiological bomb. It concluded that such a closure would result in regional impacts of $138 million in lost economic output and 1,258 person-years of lost employment.[39] The study also analyzed the potential effects of a simultaneous attack on key bridges in the port area. The study assumed such an attack would cause a longer port closure and limited truck access to the port for 120 days, and under that scenario, it estimated the national economic impact at $34 billion and 212,000 person-years of employment lost. This analysis did not consider the potential mitigating effects of other modes of transportation for moving goods out of the port (i.e., using rail instead of trucks), or potential trade diversion to other ports during the crisis.

ECONOMIC CONSEQUENCES FROM THE PSYCHOLOGICAL MARKET REACTION TO AN ATTACK COULD BE SEVERE

Finally, psychological ramifications of an attack could affect prices and supply. Researchers have noted that psychological market reactions to the consequences of an event may cause individuals and firms to change their decision-making processes, potentially causing consequences to ripple outward from the incident itself. If the incident affects key facilities, indirect effects could be magnified and also include businesses that are unable to operate both in the port and elsewhere if they are dependent on goods that move through the port. There is also the potential for unemployment of indirectly affected businesses.

The movement of gasoline prices after the *Exxon Valdez* spill is an illustration. Although the actual disruption in supply was relatively small, the oil spill sent shock waves through oil markets, particularly those most dependent on oil from the Alaskan North Slope along the West Coast. In the first week after the oil spill, spot market prices of unleaded regular gasoline increased $0.50 from $0.68 per gallon to $1.18 per gallon, a 74 percent increase due to fears of an extended closure of oil from the Alaskan North Slope. In the following weeks, however, prices began to decrease, hitting $0.99 on April 7 (2 weeks after the spill) and $0.82 on April 14 (3 weeks after the spill). Thus as markets realized that the supply shortage would be short lived, prices dropped sharply. The Department of Energy concluded in its analysis of the incident that the temporary loss of Alaskan North Slope supplies resulted in a perception of tight oil markets rather than a significant change in fundamental supply and demand factors.[40]

In: Maritime Tankers...
Editor: Thomas P. Naylor

ISBN: 978-1-60692-205-7
© 2009 Nova Science Publishers, Inc.

Chapter 4

ALTHOUGH STAKEHOLDERS ARE TAKING PROTECTIVE MEASURES, IMPLEMENTATION CHALLENGES POSE DIFFICULTY BOTH ABROAD AND AT HOME

Many efforts are under way, both internationally and domestically, to protect energy commodity tankers and their attendant facilities, but significant challenges to the success of these efforts may limit the effectiveness of these actions. These challenges are evident in protecting the loading and transit of tanker shipments. In these settings, a broad range of international stakeholders is involved, including IMO, foreign governments, vessel and facility operators, and U.S. government agencies. To help protect the international maritime supply chain, signatory governments are responsible for implementing the requirements of IMO's ISPS Code into law, many facility and vessel operators have taken steps to implement ISPS Code requirements, various industry organizations have reported security conditions in ports around the world to better inform their members, and the U.S. Coast Guard and Navy have also established their presence overseas. Challenges are evident, however, when examining how this framework has been implemented to date. Our limited reviews at foreign facilities showed wide disparity in the quality and extent of security. The Coast Guard is limited in the degree to which it can bring about improvements abroad when security is substandard, in part because its activities are limited by conditions set by host nations. The Navy takes actions that help to prevent attacks on tankers in transit, but is limited in the areas where it can patrol. In U.S. ports and waterways, a wide array of stakeholders is taking steps to protect arriving vessels, but challenges persist here as well. Key participants include the Coast Guard, CBP, and local law enforcement agencies.

In some locations, however, the Coast Guard has had difficulty meeting its own self-imposed requirements for security activity. The completion of new LNG facilities planned for a number of ports could further exacerbate the Coast Guard's ability to meet current requirements with its current resources.

IN SPITE OF THE WIDESPREAD ADOPTION OF THE ISPS CODE, THE PRIMARY CHALLENGE OVERSEAS INVOLVES OVERCOMING DISPARITIES IN SECURITY AT DIFFERENT LOCATIONS

The ISPS Code lays out the international regime for securing port facilities and commercial vessels. Signatory governments of port and flag states are responsible for ensuring compliance with the ISPS Code at port facilities and vessels under their jurisdiction. Port states enter the compliance status of their facilities directly into an IMO database. While the ISPS Code was adopted under the auspices of IMO, IMO officials told us they have no way of knowing if a country's port facilities are truly in compliance. IMO merely reports information submitted by member governments and does not verify its accuracy. Additionally, there is no other internationally recognized mechanism for third party review to verify actual compliance at port facilities. Without third party compliance review, it is extremely difficult to determine if ports are secure against terrorism.

Within some countries, the actual security measures can vary greatly from port facility to port facility, as indicated both by our own visits to foreign facilities and our discussions with agency and shipping officials. For example,

> In one country we visited, we observed varying degrees of implementation of measures to control access at different port facilities. One facility we visited had security cameras, fences, guards checking perimeter security, and identification checks for access control. Here, we were challenged by guards regularly as we passed through gates, even though facility officials were escorting us. At another facility, however, someone came to the guard station only when our escort signaled for him to come over, and fences were collapsed in some places and had holes in others.
> Vessel operators we met with also described differences in security at different ports where they load. These operators said they use many sources of intelligence to determine their security stance when entering a port. Some operators said they can call on the knowledge of their own intelligence

sources in port states, including contacts with intelligence agencies. Members of Intertanko, an international industry organization, can access its database of port security conditions, a database made up of reports from vessel operators that experience these conditions when they stop at various ports. In this database, operators reported that some ports security conditions are substantially worse than would be expected for an ISPS Code-compliant facility. In such cases, they reported taking steps that went beyond ISPS requirements, such as keeping ships at security postures beyond those called for by the port state's declared security level.

The United States is attempting to deal with facility security lapses and inconsistent security conditions in some overseas ports with overseas efforts of its own. Because of congressional concern over the effectiveness of antiterrorism measures in place at foreign ports, the Coast Guard has implemented the International Port Security Program, which was designed in part to assess and help improve the security at foreign ports. This program reviews port states' implementation of port facility security measures using established security standards, particularly the ISPS Code. According to the Coast Guard, the ISPS Code is the benchmark against which the effectiveness of a country's anti-terrorism measures will be assessed. The program also reviews the country's implementation of ship security provisions of the ISPS Code to help decide what actions to take in reviewing that country's vessels when they call in U.S. ports. Visits are conducted by Coast Guard personnel operating out of the Netherlands, Japan, Singapore, and the United States. According to program guidance, the Coast Guard officers making these visits are to exchange information with officials of the host country, visit port facilities, and share best practices.

The Coast Guard faces a number of challenges, however, in operating this program. The locations to be visited are negotiated with the host country; thus the Coast Guard team making the visit could be precluded from seeing locations that were not in compliance. Coast Guard officials said International Port Security Program officers typically make up to three visits to a country, each lasting about a week. Their assessments are thus based on conditions observed when their visits occur. We are currently conducting a separate review of the Coast Guard's international programs, and the report we issue will include a more complete review of the effectiveness of its International Port Security Program.

U.S. MILITARY PRESENCE OVERSEAS AIMED AT HELPING DETER MARITIME TERRORIST ATTACKS

In certain locations, the Navy and Coast Guard have also taken more direct action to protect oil terminals—most notably in Iraq. The Navy has set security zones (zones where unauthorized vessels will be fired upon) around Iraqi oil terminals and stationed warships and patrol boats around the terminals (see figure 8). The Navy has also stationed security personnel on the terminal platforms.

Source: U.S. Navy.

Figure 8. Tanker Approaching an Iraqi Oil Loading Terminal as U.S. Warship Patrols Nearby.

STATE DEPARTMENT OFFICIALS REVIEW CREW MEMBER VISA APPLICATIONS OVERSEAS TO PREVENT ENTRY OF TERRORISTS

An additional protective measure taken overseas is the effort of State Department (State) officials to help ensure that terrorists cannot gain entry to the United States by working as seafarers on tankers or other vessels. State Department regulations eliminated crew list visas and required all crew members seeking to enter the United States to apply for individual crew visas.[41] These visas are usually presented at U.S. ports of entry, but they can only be obtained abroad. Applicants must make appointments with State Department officials located at embassies and consulates and be interviewed. They must submit background information, fingerprints, and sufficient documentation to show they are employed by a shipping company. This information is then checked against a State Department database that contains records provided by numerous agencies and includes information on persons with visa refusals, immigration violations, criminal histories, and terrorism concerns. We reported in September 2005 steps State has taken since September 11, 2001, to improve the visa process as an antiterrorism tool as well as some of the additional actions that we believed State could take to further strengthen the process.[42] According to the State Department, it has corrective actions under way that it believes will address the recommendations.

WHILE VESSELS ARE IN TRANSIT, THE PRIMARY CHALLENGE INVOLVES PATROLLING THE VAST DISTANCES INVOLVED

Many countries help to protect energy commodity tankers by patrolling the sea transit routes. For example, Combined Task Force 150, which as of December 2006 included navies of the United States, Canada, France, Germany, Italy, Pakistan, and the United Kingdom, conducted operations in the Arabian Sea, Gulf of Oman, Gulf of Aden, Indian Ocean, and Red Sea to secure the waterways and prevent piracy and terrorism (see figure 9).[43] Naval and coast guard forces of Indonesia, Malaysia, and Singapore patrol the Strait of Malacca, a major choke point in the shipment of energy commodities. Improvements in security in the strait led to its removal from a list of areas in which Lloyds vessel insurers could raise premiums due to severe security risks. To protect their ships in areas of known danger, tanker operators said they are also modifying their normal practices. For example, tanker operators told us that they have directed their vessels to travel much further off the shore of Somalia than they would ordinarily. Near Somalia, the International Maritime Bureau recommended in 2005 that commercial vessels stay 200 miles away from the coast, and the U.S. Maritime Administration and Coast Guard issued similar guidance for U.S.-flagged vessels. In piracy-prone waters, such as the Strait of Malacca, actions include sailing with all lights on, using extra lookouts, and equipping crews with fire hoses to prevent or repel boarders.

Source: U.S. Navy.

Figure 9. U.S. Warship Engaging Suspected Pirate Vessel near Somalia.

While these actions have had some success in securing transit routes, the vast areas to be patrolled and the small number of ships available present the military forces of the world with great challenges in protecting the sea lanes. For example, a multinational task force of military vessels that patrols the Arabian Sea, Gulf of Oman, Gulf of Aden, and northwestern Indian Ocean is made up of about 15 ships. The navies of regional countries also patrol near their shores, but in areas such as the Horn of Africa this multinational task force is the only major presence. Because tankers travel so frequently and so few naval ships are available to be on station, naval protection cannot be offered for all those who travel in these waters.

Besides patrolling the waters, tracking the movement of tankers is another way to monitor them. A recently passed IMO requirement calls for most commercial vessels, including tankers, to begin transmitting identification and location information on or before December 31, 2008, to SOLAS contracting governments under certain specified circumstances. This will allow the vessels to be tracked over the course of their voyages. Under this requirement, information on the ship's identity, location, date, and time of the position will be made available to the ship's flag state, the ship's destination port state, and any coastal state within 1,000 miles of the ship's route. For ships approaching the United States, an extensive tracking program is already in place. The Coast Guard currently tracks ships as they approach the U.S. coastline and is developing programs for longer-range tracking.[44]

IN U.S. WATERWAYS AND PORTS, THE PRIMARY CHALLENGE INVOLVES COPING WITH LIMITED RESOURCES AND A GROWING SECURITY WORKLOAD

Domestically, many agencies and other stakeholders have taken steps to develop and implement plans for helping ensure the security of maritime energy commodity shipments. The Coast Guard's primary challenge is utilizing its limited resources to meet its security workload. Since the terrorist attacks of September 11, 2001, Coast Guard field units have seen a substantial increase in their security workload.[45] Coast Guard field units at some ports have not always been able to meet their maritime security activity requirements. Moreover, the Coast Guard's resource demands are expected to grow as more facilities for importing LNG come on line, increasing the number of shipments requiring Coast Guard protection.

The efforts to provide security over energy commodity shipments arriving at U.S. waterways and port facilities involve a wide range of federal and local agencies as well as owners and operators of the facilities that receive the shipments. Much of the framework for port security is contained in MTSA. DHS, which is the main agency responsible for homeland security responsibilities contained in MTSA, has assigned most of the responsibilities to the Coast Guard.[46] To carry out this responsibility, as well as the nation's port state oversight of foreign-flagged vessels, the Coast Guard's efforts range from boarding ships and escorting those shipments of greatest concern to patrolling port waters and overseeing the security actions undertaken by vessel and facility operators. CBP has the lead role in ensuring that only authorized persons onboard tankers come ashore when calling on U.S. ports and that no contraband is smuggled into the United States using the tankers.[47] MTSA requires regular vulnerability assessments of port facilities, and facility owners and operators are required to develop and update regularly a plan for meeting basic security requirements. Facility security plans and updates to them are to be reviewed and approved by DHS.

Security Requirements Vary by Commodity

Particularly for the Coast Guard, the security activities vary greatly depending on the type of energy commodity being carried by tankers. Two energy commodities, LNG and LPG, are on the list of what the Coast Guard has traditionally called Certain Dangerous Cargo (CDC).[48] Coast Guard guidance requires its field units to take certain actions to protect LNG and LPG tankers in key port areas, which include high-population areas or areas with critical infrastructure, such as bridges or refineries.[49] Beyond protecting LNG and LPG shipments in these key port areas, Coast Guard field units are required to implement security activities commensurate with the extent of critical infrastructure, extent of high-profile vessel traffic transiting through key port areas, and availability of support of non-Coast Guard entities, such as state and local law enforcement agencies. According to senior Coast Guard field officials with LNG security responsibilities, LNG tanker transits have received the greatest attention of the two, due in large part to the much greater size of LNG tankers, the amount of hazardous cargo they are carrying, and the public perception of the danger of LNG shipments. Many of these security measures are now being implemented at existing LNG ports around the country. The security measures address two phases of LNG operations, including (1) the transit of an underway tanker through a port and (2) the period when a tanker is moored at a receiving terminal.

Source: Distrigas of Massachusetts © 2006.

Figure 10. Safety and Security Escort for LNG Tanker.

Source: GAO.

Figure 11. Coast Guard Enforcing Security Zone around Moored LNG Tanker.

Coast Guard security activity requirements are less stringent for oil tankers or tankers carrying many other petroleum-based products, such as gasoline or crude oil, because they are not identified in the CDC list of hazardous marine cargo as posing the greatest human safety risks. However, field units do have discretion to take additional actions to protect oil tankers and associated waterside loading facilities that are determined to pose security concerns.

State and Local Law Enforcement Agencies Play a Major Role in the Protection of Tankers and Facilities

At many ports we visited or contacted, Coast Guard field units are receiving assistance from state and local law enforcement agencies for help in conducting port security operations.[50] These partnerships with state and local law enforcement agencies have been encouraged by Coast Guard headquarters. Coast Guard officials said the support has been particularly valuable in protecting LNG carriers. For example, field units at two of the four ports with onshore LNG importing facilities reported using regular escort support from state or local law enforcement agencies.

In addition to state and local law enforcement agencies, facility operators play a significant role in protecting against terrorist threats. For those key energy ports we visited, the Coast Guard reported that the waterfront energy facilities in those ports were taking actions to comply with the requirements the Coast Guard established pursuant to MTSA. Of the 19 domestic waterside petroleum facilities we visited, all were reported by the Coast Guard to be in compliance with MTSA regulations. Examples of steps taken include key-card access systems, closed-circuit television cameras and sensors along fencing, hardened perimeter fencing, and reinforced gates at most access control points. Facility operators told us they conduct regular security drills involving emergency and terrorism scenarios and they regularly share pertinent security information with other participants of the Area Maritime Security Committees.[51] In some cases we observed steps that go beyond MTSA requirements, such as using radio frequency identification cards that can track the location of all persons on facility property.

The Coast Guard Faces Challenges Meeting Internal Security Guidance

Coast Guard records show that its field units in several of the energy-related ports we reviewed have been unable to accomplish many of the port security responsibilities called for in Coast Guard guidance. According to the data we obtained and our discussions with field unit officials, resource shortfalls were the primary reasons for not meeting these responsibilities.

The Coast Guard's Near-Term Efforts to Align Requirements with Field Unit Capacity Have Limitations

We have noted in earlier work that the Coast Guard is ahead of many agencies in the degree to which it has developed a sound framework for managing its workload on the basis of risk.[52] When carried out effectively, risk management offers a way to make informed decisions about how best to use limited resources. In the Coast Guard's case, its actions involve a balancing act both in deciding how best to meet its various security and nonsecurity missions agencywide, but also in weighing the pros and cons of investing additional resources in energy commodity tanker protection versus the wider range of other port activities that require protection. The Coast Guard uses the requirements laid out in its guidance to establish a port-specific security approach in which the workload varies based on such factors as the proximity of population centers to the port area, the extent of critical infrastructure at the port, the extent of high-profile vessel traffic transiting through key port areas, and the availability of support from other entities.

Given that the resource levels of some field units have limited their ability to achieve Coast Guard security standards, the Coast Guard has attempted to realign its security requirements to more closely match available resource levels. Coast Guard headquarters officials meet on an annual basis to review new risk assessments and current Coast Guard capacity to mitigate risk. The Coast Guard also receives recommendations from field unit commanders for introducing tactical efficiencies into security requirements. Over the past several years, the Coast Guard has revised its operational security guidance in two main ways:

Revising the standards for the amount of activity required for conducting some security activities. In August 2006 the Coast Guard substantially reduced the types of CDC-carrying vessels that must be escorted. The Coast Guard developed a subset list of the CDC commodities—called Especially Hazardous Cargo—it determined as posing the greatest safety and security risks. This list included both LNG and LPG, meaning that the activities required to protect them remain unchanged. However, for CDC commodities not included on the Especially Hazardous Cargo list, such as vinyl chloride, escort requirements were eliminated during normal threat conditions— MARSEC I.[53] In all, requirements were reduced for about 20 different CDC commodities carried in bulk. The August 2006 list of Especially Hazardous Cargo consisted of seven hazardous liquid gas or liquid commodities: acrylonitrile, ammonium nitrate, ammonium nitrate/fuel oil, anhydrous ammonia, chlorine, LNG, and LPG.

Providing greater operational flexibility for Area Commanders when resource constraints may limit the ability to meet requirements. The Coast Guard has introduced new tactical options that Area Commanders may utilize, in some cases, to accomplish resource intensive security activities.

The Coast Guard's methodology used to develop the Especially Hazardous Cargo has two substantial shortcomings, however. Our specific concerns are as follows:

Lack of thoroughness. To identify the highest risk CDC commodities, senior Coast Guard headquarters officials told us they reviewed available consequence analysis assessments that had been conducted by the Coast Guard's Special Technical Assessment Program and also reviewed a 2004 consequence analysis of LNG by Sandia National Laboratories.[54] They said they also incorporated the views of persons with expertise in CDC commodities, including Coast Guard field officials. However, the Coast Guard did not perform consequence assessments on many CDC commodities by the time it created the Especially Hazardous Cargo list, and as of January 1, 2007, it still had not done so.

No systematic comparative analysis was conducted to identify and prioritize the highest-consequence commodities. Coast Guard headquarters officials acknowledged they did not conduct a relative risk assessment of the CDC commodities. Rather, officials told us they relied on the collective best judgment of Coast Guard experts from field units and headquarters that had significant experience dealing with various transportable energy and chemical commodities. By conducting a relative risk analysis of all CDC commodities, the Coast Guard would have had available more definitive input for determining which CDC vessels posed the greatest risks necessitating additional mitigation measures, which in this case would be an escort.

The Coast Guard is taking action to address the methodological limitations we note. Shortly after the Coast Guard released the Especially Hazardous Cargo list, we shared our concerns with Coast Guard officials. The Coast Guard has since begun efforts to broaden its studies of potential consequences to include a wide range of hazardous commodities. It contracted with the American Bureau of Shipping to perform a comparative analysis of the consequences of an attack on vessels carrying all commodities on the CDC list, including LNG and LPG. The product of this analysis is to be a ranking of the relative consequences of each of the CDC commodities. This study is scheduled to be completed in spring 2007. Coast Guard headquarters officials told us that following this analysis, and subject to available funding and other considerations, they may consider adding other commodities to the comparative analysis, such as gasoline and jet fuel.

Going beyond the consequence analyses of hazardous commodities, the Coast Guard has also developed a tool to compare the overall relative risk scores of different terrorist attacks at the nation's ports. Field units are developing risk scenarios for potential targets at their ports and possible attack types that could be used against those targets. Using the Maritime Security Risk Assessment Model, the units are to analyze the different risk scenarios in relation to three key elements of risk: reported threat of different types of attack, vulnerability of the targets (incorporating different protective actions taken by security stakeholders), and consequences of a successful attack (including human health, economic, and environmental).[55] Each risk scenario is to receive a score. These risk scores are to be comparable within and between ports so that they can be used in risk management decisions both locally and nationally.

ADDITIONAL LNG FACILITIES SET TO COME ON LINE WILL LIKELY POSE ADDITIONAL CHALLENGES FOR MEETING MISSION REQUIREMENTS

In the longer term, plans for adding additional LNG facilities may require the Coast Guard to reassess its workload yet again. Currently the Coast Guard is faced with providing security for vessels arriving at four domestic onshore LNG import facilities, but the number of LNG tankers bringing shipments to these facilities will increase considerably because of expansions that are planned or under way.[56] In addition, industry analysts expect approximately 12 more LNG facilities will be built over the next decade (see figure 12). Consequently, Coast Guard field units will likely be required to significantly expand their security workloads to conduct new LNG security missions.

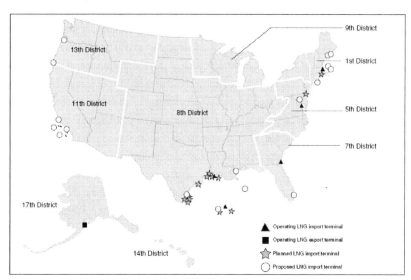

Source: Federal Energy Regulatory Commission and GAO.

Figure 12. Location of Operating, Planned, and Proposed LNG Marine Terminals by U.S. Coast Guard District.

Recognizing this coming increase in demand on security resources at LNG ports, Coast Guard field units have been planning strategies to help meet this demand. We found evidence that, in their planning efforts, Coast Guard field units and affected locations are seeking assistance from a wide range of stakeholders and sources. In particular, stakeholders mentioned the following:

Manpower from state and local law enforcement. Several field units plan to rely on state and local agencies to conduct a considerable share of the new LNG workloads. While state and local law enforcement agencies have generally agreed to participate in LNG security operations, such support was largely contingent upon their receiving funding to cover their own resource gaps. According to the Coast Guard, at some ports, law enforcement agencies required funding to cover new capital investments, such as additional patrol boats, as well as operational costs such as funding for additional manpower or fuel for the new boats.

Financial help from facility operators. At some of the proposed LNG ports we reviewed, facility operators were also planning to contribute considerable financial resources to help fund new LNG security operations. In doing so, these companies planned to fund both operational and capital enhancement costs for state and local law enforcement agencies that had agreed in concept to support Coast Guard LNG security missions. At two ports where the Coast Guard had approved security arrangements for new LNG facilities, state and local law enforcement agencies had already developed, or were planning to develop, a cost-sharing agreement with the facilities. For example, at one port, a potential LNG facility operator made a commitment to fund most of the capital enhancements and operational costs of the state and local law enforcement agencies involved, including two patrol boats for state agencies, two tugboats, and communications equipment. Facility operators told us they were motivated to provide resources because they understood that doing so was essential to ensuring final approval of the LNG facilities. Some facility operators also told us that the Energy Policy Act of 2005 required them to develop resource cost-sharing agreements to offset state and local government resources used specifically for the new LNG facilities.[57]

Financial help through federal grants. State and local law enforcement agencies also reported that they were relying, in part, on federal grants to obtain additional resources. Of the 15 state and local law enforcement agencies we contacted, 9 agencies reported applying for Port Security Grants or Urban Area Security Initiative grants. Law enforcement agency officials told us they planned to fund capital enhancements with this grant funding.

Among those items officials planned to fund with their grants were new patrol boats, construction of a new boathouse and piers, helicopters, and security cameras to be placed along an LNG transit route.

While port security grants and resource sharing agreements are expected to address at least part of the resource needs of the Coast Guard's law enforcement partners, the Coast Guard is likely to require additional resources to fulfill its own new security responsibilities. To date, however, field units have made little progress in obtaining additional resources. Additionally, because federal law prohibits the Coast Guard from receiving resources for its own use from private sector companies, the Coast Guard cannot use resource-sharing partnerships to help fill its own resource needs. Consequently, Coast Guard headquarters officials told us they recognize that despite the efforts of Captains of the Port to develop local solutions to new security demands, some field units will continue to lack the resources necessary to meet their increasing LNG security workloads.

Coast Guard headquarters officials told us they were considering two general options to provide field units with the necessary resources to carry out their new LNG security workloads. These two options are as follows:

Redistribute resources to units with new LNG activity. Coast Guard officials told us they are considering shifting resources from ports with surplus resources to ports with new or expanded LNG facilities. Coast Guard headquarters officials told us, however, that they have not yet determined which ports would, or even could, provide these excess resources. Coast Guard's Atlantic area—where most of the new LNG activity is expected—has ordered districts and field units to report any excess resource capacity. Guided by risk management, Coast Guard headquarters may redistribute any available excess capacity to ports with new LNG security workloads. The earliest that the Coast Guard could reprogram assets from within the Atlantic Area is fiscal year 2009.

Request new resources via budget proposals. Coast Guard officials also reported that they may request additional funding through the annual budget process to support the acquisition of additional boats and personnel to conduct vessel escorts and infrastructure patrols and the training of additional personnel.

As of January 1, 2007, Coast Guard headquarters officials told us they had not yet developed a plan—or blueprint—for how to proceed with these two options for addressing new LNG security resource demands. The decisions about how to proceed may involve difficult choices, because shifting resources to this growing need could involve trimming resources now tasked to other homeland security duties or traditional non-homeland security missions, and because seeking more resources involves asking Coast Guard decision makers to weigh important, but competing, priorities. A national plan that identifies the Coast Guard's nationwide LNG resource needs and identifies milestones and funding needs for meeting those needs can help the Coast Guard manage its limited resources and communicate resource needs to Congress. It is important to complete this plan and address in it key elements and issues so that it is both comprehensive and useful to decision makers who must make difficult policy and budget choices.

In: Maritime Tankers...
Editor: Thomas P. Naylor

ISBN: 978-1-60692-205-7
© 2009 Nova Science Publishers, Inc.

Chapter 5

STAKEHOLDERS HAVE DEVELOPED SPILL AND TERRORISM RESPONSE PLANS BUT FACE SEVERAL CHALLENGES IN INTEGRATING THEM

To mitigate the consequences of a terrorist attack on a tanker carrying energy commodities, the United States has multiple plans that address actions to be taken at the national, port, facility, and vessel levels. To translate these plans into effective response actions, stakeholders could face at least three main challenges. First, if an attack were to occur, the stakeholders would need to integrate current, separate plans for the two types of responses necessary for mitigating the consequences of an attack—spill and terrorism responses. Second, port-level plans to mitigate the potentially substantial economic consequences of an attack, such as plans that set priorities for the movement of vessels after a port reopens, could be useful. Third, stakeholders may need to obtain resources to ensure that they can carry out the plans. At the port level, this challenge may extend to response equipment, training, and communications equipment. To date, federal grants for port security have been directed mostly to prevention rather than response, but now DHS is moving toward a more comprehensive risk-based decision-making process for allocating grant funds. At the time of our review, DHS did not have performance measures for determining how to allocate resources to ensure ports can effectively respond to an energy commodities spill caused by terrorism.

PLANNING FOR SPILL RESPONSE IS LARGELY SEPARATE FROM PLANNING FOR TERRORISM RESPONSE

The planning framework for responding to spills and terrorism incidents is extensive, involving multiple federal plans and memorandums of understanding, port-specific plans, as well as plans for individual facilities and vessels. As figure 13 shows, at the national level these plans are carried out under the general framework of the National Response Plan (NRP) but are developed into two separate lines of effort—one for spill response, the other for terrorism response.

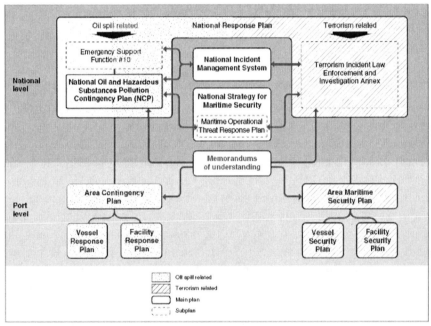

Source: GAO.

Figure 13. Relationship of Spill and Terrorism Response Plans and Agreements.

The NRP designates the Coast Guard as the primary agency for spill response on water and the FBI as the primary agency for terrorism response, and it calls on the two agencies to coordinate their responses if the terrorist attack involves energy commodities. For this type of incident, FBI officials stated, crime scene investigation and preservation would take place at the same time as the environmental response activities that would be initiated to contain the likely spill. In this situation, the NRP notes that spill responders will provide assistance, investigative support, and intelligence analysis for oil and hazardous materials response in coordination with the law enforcement and criminal investigation activities of the FBI.

As the figure shows, beneath the NRP, spill responses are coordinated by the National Oil and Hazardous Substances Pollution Contingency Plan (NCP), while terrorism responses are coordinated by the Terrorism Incident Law Enforcement and Investigation Annex.[58] Also at the federal level, various other federal plans and agreements, such as the National Incident Management System (NIMS), the Marine Operational Threat Response Plan (MOTR), and interagency memorandums of agreement also help guide the response. The spill and terrorism responses continue into port-level planning, where the key guidance for spill responses is found in a port's Area Contingency Plan (ACP) and the key guidance for terrorism responses is found in the port's Area Maritime Security Plan (AMSP). Table 3 provides a brief description of the various plans and agreements found in figure 13.

Table 3. Federal and Port-level Plans and Agreements Governing Response to Spills on Water and Terrorist Attacks

Plans and agreements	Description
Federal plans and agreements	
National Response Plan (NRP)	As the umbrella plan for federal response, it provides a structure for plans at the national and local levels. It also incorporates interagency plans for responding to spills and terrorist attacks. If a terrorist attack results in an energy commodity spill, calls for the Coast Guard and FBI to coordinate their response efforts, with the FBI as lead agency.
Emergency Support Function #10: National Oil and Hazardous Substances Pollution Contingency Plan (NCP)	Lays out planning and operational activities at the federal and port levels for spills, and designates the Coast Guard as the lead federal agency for spills on water. The Coast Guard has entered into agreements to coordinate spill response activities with at least 16 federal departments and agencies, (e.g., the Department of Defense may provide assistance through its Supervisor of Salvage and Diving).
Terrorism Incident Law Enforcement and Investigation Annex	Provides guidance for how federal agencies are to coordinate with state and local responders. References federal terrorism response policies, priorities (with public safety receiving top priority), and tasks to be performed in responding to an attack, such as setting up interagency command and communications groups. Identifies the FBI as responsible for coordinating and conducting all federal law enforcement and criminal investigation activities after a terrorist attack.

Table 3. (Continued).

Plans and agreements	Description
National Strategy for Maritime Security	Designed to integrate and synchronize existing department-level strategies to ensure their effective and efficient implementation, as well as align all federal government maritime security programs and initiatives into a comprehensive and cohesive national effort.
Maritime Operational Threat Response Plan (MOTR)	Aids coordination of U.S. government response to threats against the United States and its interests in the maritime domain by establishing roles and responsibilities for government response.
National Incident Management System (NIMS)	Used by the NRP as the framework for standard incident command and management processes, protocols, and procedures for federal responses to any incident, including terrorism, and outlines coordination steps.
Memorandums of understanding (MOU)	1979: Agreement between the Coast Guard and FBI, aimed at ensuring coordinated efforts, eliminating delays in response time, and ensuring continued development of procedures and contingency plans. 2002: Agreement between the Coast Guard, Department of Justice, and other members of the National Response Team, aimed at facilitating coordination of criminal investigations, enforcement, and environmental response activities.[a]
Port-level plans Area Contingency Plan (ACP)	Describes what needs to be protected in the event of an emergency and how to protect it, what resources are available to respond, and the desired outcomes from the spill response.
Facility Response Plan (FRP)	Describes how the facility will respond to, contain, and clean up a spill.
Vessel Response Plan (VRP)	Describes how the vessel will respond to, contain, and clean up a spill.
Area Maritime Security Plan (AMSP)	Describes how port stakeholders will deter a terrorist attack or other transportation security incident, or secure the port in the event such an attack occurs.
Facility Security Plan (FSP)	Describes how the facility will prevent an incident and secure the facility when an attack occurs at the facility or on a vessel docked at the facility.
Vessel Security Plan (VSP)	Describes how the vessel will prevent an incident and secure the vessel when an attack occurs on the vessel.

Source: GAO's analysis of federal and port-level plans and agreements.

[a] The U.S. National Response Team (NRT) is an organization of 16 federal departments and agencies responsible for coordinating emergency preparedness and response to oil and hazardous substance pollution incidents. The NRT is a planning and coordinating body under the National Contingency Plan and provides national-level policy guidance prior to an incident.

At the federal level, in addition to the plans and agreements governing spill and terrorism responses in table 3, other guidance and requirements related to economic recovery include the following:

The Maritime Infrastructure Recovery Plan (MIRP)—a supporting plan for the National Strategy for Maritime Security—contains procedures for managing the economic consequences and recovery of maritime infrastructure after a transportation security incident, such as a terrorist attack. The MIRP provides strategic-level guidance for national, regional, and local decisionmakers to set priorities for restoring the flow of domestic cargo. The plan recommends that the Captain of the Port consider key shipping channels and waterways for homeland security; military traffic; and commercial operations; key landside transportation infrastructure, such as tunnels and bridges; and other infrastructure key to maintaining continuity of operations in the port.
The SAFE Port Act of 2006 requires the Secretary of Homeland Security to develop protocols for the resumption of trade after a transportation security incident, such as a terrorist attack.[59] The protocols must include a plan to redeploy resources and personnel as necessary to reestablish the flow of trade, and appropriate factors for establishing prioritization of vessels and cargo that are critical for response and recovery, including factors related to public health, national security, and economic need.

At the port level, under the Oil Pollution Act of 1990 and the Maritime Transportation Security Act of 2002, the Captain of the Port is to establish both spill and terrorism response plans.[60] In doing so, the Captain of the Port must identify local public and private port stakeholders who will develop and revise separate plans for marine spills of oil and hazardous materials (ACP) and for terrorism response (AMSP). Both plans call for coordinated implementation with other plans, such as the response and security plans developed by specific facilities or vessels. Local stakeholders are organized into two separate groups: an area committee for spill response (Area Committee), which develops the ACP, and an area committee for terrorism response (Area Maritime Security Committee), which develops the AMSP—both committees are chaired by the Captain of the Port. Some stakeholders, such as port authorities, fire departments, and facilities in the port, may be part of both committees, while others may be part of only one committee. For example, oil spill response organizations are likely to be involved only with spill response planning.

If an energy commodity tanker was attacked while moving through a U.S. port or while docked, a range of response activities would need to occur to address the consequences. Figure 14 illustrates how incident response would potentially take place following an attack and a subsequent spill.

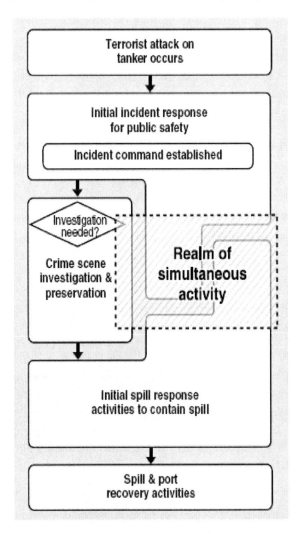

Source: GAO.

Figure 14. Incident Response Sequence When an Attack Occurs Resulting in a Spill.

As figure 14 shows, incident response includes three separate but overlapping activities, as reported by port stakeholders:

Initial incident response for public safety and establishment of the incident command site. Because energy commodity tankers carry flammable and/or hazardous materials, the first responders are likely to be area fire and police departments; receiving facility personnel may also respond. The first concern is always public safety, and therefore the fire department would begin rescuing victims and addressing the probable fire. Law enforcement agencies would secure the perimeter of the scene to prevent potential follow-on attacks as well as to prevent the public from moving too close to the attack location—both to protect the public and to maintain the crime scene for subsequent investigation. Initial responders would also establish a multi-agency incident command site near the location of the vessel, where all responding agencies with jurisdictional responsibilities for spill and terrorism response would congregate to manage the operations.

Crime scene preservation and investigation, and initial spill response activities. As public safety operations continue, law enforcement agencies would determine whether terrorism had caused the spill, and if so, would conduct an investigation at the same time that life safety operations are continuing and spill response operations are beginning. Investigations would involve crime scene and perimeter control, determining if additional devices may be present and disposing of them, and apprehending suspects. Spill operations would initially involve the laying of a containment boom to protect the surrounding environment from contamination caused by the spill. Law enforcement and spill response organizations will need to coordinate their activities because actions to mitigate environmental consequences can potentially damage crime scene evidence.

Spill and port recovery activities. Once the resulting spill is contained, incident commanders would determine their next steps, depending on conditions. Spill recovery may include intentionally burning contained oil, allowing the commodity to evaporate, using chemicals to disperse the spill, or using mechanical recovery to skim the oil out of the water. If a terrorist attack had occurred, the crime scene investigation would have to be conducted before the port could be fully restored for cargo and passenger ships.

According to FBI officials, the FBI would work with the Coast Guard to get access to the incident site as soon as possible to obtain all crime scene evidence possible, without interfering with the response.

These complex activities would be carried out by many different federal, state, and local agencies. Figure 15 illustrates one possible scenario for spill and terrorism response actions and shows some of the agencies that might carry out these actions.

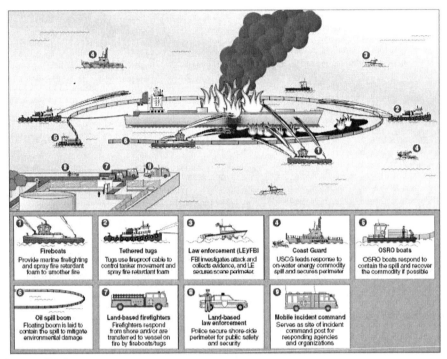

Source: GAO.

Figure 15. Potential Actions Taken to Respond to an Attack on an Energy Commodity Tanker.

FEDERAL AGENCIES AND LOCAL PORTS COULD FACE CHALLENGES IN INTEGRATING SPILL AND TERRORISM RESPONSE PLANS, PLANNING FOR ECONOMIC RESPONSE, AND OBTAINING NEEDED RESOURCES

In the event of a terrorist attack on an energy commodity tanker, federal agencies and port communities could face challenges in integrating their spill and terrorism response plans. Ports could face two additional challenges: planning for economic response activities and obtaining the necessary resources to respond to a terrorist attack on an energy commodity tanker.

Federal Agencies and Ports Could Face Challenges in Integrating Spill and Terrorism Response Plans

As we have noted in prior reports, a fundamental goal of emergency preparation and response is the ability to respond to emergency incidents of any size or cause with well-planned, well-coordinated, and effective efforts that reduce the loss of life and property and set the stage for recovery. In our September 2006 report on the preparation for and response to Hurricane Katrina, we stated that fundamental to effective preparation and response are (1) clearly defined, clearly communicated, and clearly understood legal authorities, responsibilities, and roles at the federal, state, and local level, and (2) identification and development of the capabilities needed to mount a well-coordinated, effective response to reduce the loss of life and property and set the stage for recovery. Providing these fundamentals requires effective planning and coordination, including detailed operational plans, and robust training and exercises in which needed capabilities are realistically tested, assessed, and problems identified and addressed.[61] With regard to potential attacks on energy commodity tankers in U.S. ports, the ports could face challenges if roles and responsibilities have not been clearly defined, communicated, and understood and if needed capabilities have not been fully identified and appropriately tested. The National Preparedness Goal uses 15 scenarios to identify 37 capabilities and the associated critical tasks needed to respond to incidents of national significance—those that go beyond the state and local levels and require a coordinated federal response. However, the scenarios used to identify these capabilities do not specifically encompass the capabilities needed for responding to attacks on oil, gas, or other tankers in American ports.

The NRP calls upon the Coast Guard and the FBI to coordinate their response in the event of a terrorist attack on an oil or hazardous materials tanker. However, the agencies cannot be assured that their joint response, concurrently implementing the numerous existing plans, will be effective unless they have developed a detailed operational plan that integrates their spill and terrorism responses and have tested these responses in joint exercises. According to headquarters and field office Coast Guard and FBI officials, coordination would be managed through the use of the unified command structure in the National Incident Management System and the other general coordination mechanisms in the NRP and the MOTR. However, the unified command structure and the NRP are generally not specific in explaining how they will be made operational following an attack. As we have recently reported, the implementation of the NRP following Hurricane Katrina identified concerns with coordination within and between federal government entities using the plan.[62] We recommended the development of detailed operational plans for the NRP and its annexes.[63]

In addition to having operational plans, agencies should conduct joint exercises that simulate an attack and the agencies' responses.[64] Without such exercises, it would be questionable whether joint Coast Guard and FBI activities would proceed as planned. Simulation exercises help determine the strengths and weaknesses of various plans and the ability of multiple agencies or communities to respond to an emergency incident. According to DHS's Homeland Security Exercise and Evaluation Program, well-designed and executed exercises are the most effective means of (1) testing and validating policies, plans, procedures, training, equipment, and interagency agreements; (2) clarifying and training personnel in roles and responsibilities; (3) improving interagency coordination and communications; (4) identifying gaps in resources; (5) improving individual performance; and (6) identifying opportunities for improvement.

The value of joint simulation exercises in uncovering problems has been demonstrated in the results of the largest national, state, and local interagency terrorism response exercise ever conducted. This exercise—called TOPOFF 3—was conducted in April 2005 and included explosions and hazardous materials releases in multiple locations around the nation (none of which were on the water). According to the Coast Guard after-action report for one of the sites, the FBI (1) never fully integrated into and accepted the unified command called for under NIMS, (2) did not appropriately staff the incident command post with its representatives, (3) maintained distinctions between hazardous materials release response and terrorism investigation actions, and (4) kept management of the investigation separate from the incident management overseen by the unified command. According to the after-action report, "concurrent management of both the investigation and all other response functions would have increased the effectiveness and efficiency of the response effort." The report also recommended the continuation of multiagency training and exercises to test interagency coordination efforts.

The need for joint spill and terrorism response exercises has been discussed, but exercises have not been conducted, at the national level. Specifically, planning discussions for the 2004 Spill of National Significance (SONS) exercise identified the need to clarify how the FBI fits into spill response activities when the possibility of terrorism is present, but the exercise did not test integrating the FBI's and other agencies' response.[65] However, both Coast Guard guidance and the Department of Justice's Inspector General have supported the need to combine spill and terrorism response exercises. Specifically:

> Coast Guard guidance recommends combining terrorism response exercises with other exercises, such as spill response. OPA 90 and MTSA implementing regulations require similar schedules for exercises of spill and terrorism response plans, and the integration of these exercises could improve response performance and complete required multiple response exercise mandates at one time, according to Coast Guard officials.
> The Department of Justice's Inspector General in 2006 called for more joint exercises between the Coast Guard and the FBI in high-risk ports to, among other things, resolve potential role and incident command conflicts in the event of a maritime terrorism incident.[66] The Inspector General's report emphasized the interaction of Coast Guard and FBI security units, but these recommendations are equally applicable for integrated exercises to respond to a spill caused by a terrorist attack. Once public safety is addressed, the Coast Guard and FBI have different priorities for their jurisdictional responsibilities—spill containment and cleanup and crime scene preservation and investigation, respectively. At the time of our review, FBI officials told us they knew of no upcoming joint planned exercises. FBI headquarters officials have not issued guidance to field office agents on integrating spill and terrorism responses activities within a single exercise.

Coast Guard officials told us that the MOTR is intended to delineate Coast Guard and FBI roles in responding to an attack. FBI headquarters officials told us that their participation in several MOTR conference calls demonstrated that coordination among MOTR agencies is effective. These telephone discussions may improve overall coordination, but exercises for joint spill and terrorism responses should be conducted as often as appropriate.[67]

At the port level, effectively integrating spill and terrorism emergency responses requires all plans to operate in unison—the port spill response plan (ACP) and the port terrorism response plan (AMSP), as well as facility and vessel response plans. As figure 13 shows, there is no direct operational link between the ACP and the AMSP.

Without a direct link, spill responders may not have the information they need to respond to a spill caused by a terrorist attack. While the AMSP has served as the terrorism response plan for ports since July 2004, it contains sensitive security information and is therefore only available to those individuals who are considered to have a "need to know." As a result, nonsecurity personnel, such oil spill cleanup responders, may not have access to these plans during an emergency. For example, only 3 of the 13 ports we visited had ACPs that addressed terrorism response within the spill plan by incorporating terrorism incident annexes or other plans. Consequently, the ACPs may need to have explicit sections for responding to terrorism.[68]

The general lack of integration in the plans carries over to the separate spill and terrorism response communities at the port level. As previously discussed, individual members on these committees may not know all the members of the other committee, but a terrorist attack on a tanker would require them to respond simultaneously. We identified only a few examples of joint committee meetings that enabled members to interact. For example, Coast Guard officials told us that, since September 11, 2001, the Captain of the Port at one location has facilitated meetings between spill response providers and local offices of emergency management and federal and local law enforcement agencies in order to improve response coordination among all entities. They stated that if the spill and terrorism response communities were formally joined, response integration and efficiency would improve. In addition, at another location, Coast Guard officials noted, the local area training and exercise workgroup contains members of both the spill and terrorism response committees in order to consolidate training and exercises. Finally, in an attempt to improve communication, the FBI established Maritime Liaison Agents (MLA) at the ports so that all stakeholders would know the local agent in the event of an incident.[69] At some ports we visited the spill responders knew who the FBI agent was and at other ports they said they did not.

USCG guidance states that local port operators, municipalities, and public safety agencies are expected to provide and maintain adequate disaster response capabilities in their ports, with capability requirements likely to vary from port to port depending on size, commodities received, environmental considerations, relation to population, etc. Recognizing the variability of capability requirements, the USCG has developed Critical Success Factors (CSF) for spill response that drive a "Best Possible Response"—that is, a set of general goals to achieve when conducting a comprehensive and effective response. Six particular CSF are to be considered when developing ACPs, including (1) no public or responder injuries, illness or deaths; (2) sensitive areas protected; (3) resource damage minimized; (4) infrastructure damage minimized; (5) economic impact minimized; and (6) highly coordinated law enforcement and emergency management operations. Joint exercises can maximize the ability of a given port to carry out a "best response" in the event of an attack on a tanker. However, we recognize that numerous scenarios could be exercised in any given port; consequently, joint spill and terrorism response exercises may not be the most urgent for a port that receives limited quantities of energy commodities. Figure 16 shows firefighters preparing for a potential marine response during a training exercise.

Source: GAO.

Figure 16. Firefighters Preparing for a Maritime Terrorism Training Exercise.

Two developments—one a project at an individual port, the other a new requirement added by Congress—may help bring about more integrated responses. Specifically:

At one port, we found a potential leading practice for integrating a marine terrorism response. The port's Marine Terrorism Response (MTR) project was launched to develop and validate a multiagency response system and national model plan to help mobilize local, state, and federal resources for marine terrorism incidents. The MTR's goals include increasing preparedness, identifying gaps in emergency response capabilities, and planning for timely restoration of trade. The project generated a response plan and a field guide for how to integrate responses for a range of issues, such as public safety, response coordination, recovery, and crime scene management. Stakeholders plan to incorporate existing response plans, such as the ACP, as annexes to the MTR. According to the FBI official involved with the MTR planning process, the MTR serves as an effective linkage between the spill and terrorism response sections of the National Response Plan.[70]

Under the SAFE Port Act of 2006, DHS must develop interagency operational centers by fall 2009 for port security at all high-priority ports. The Coast Guard and the FBI are among the agencies that will be represented at these operational centers, as will other public and private sector stakeholders who would be adversely affected by a terrorist attack. These centers may also include stakeholders who would be involved in a joint spill and terrorism response. Integration may be improved through the daily interaction of all these stakeholders. In April 2006 testimony before the House Homeland Security Committee, DHS's Deputy Secretary stated that physically connecting the various agencies involved is important, and the Port of New York and New Jersey's Manager of Port Security voiced support for the development of joint operation centers in key U.S. ports.[71]

PORT PLANS TO MITIGATE ECONOMIC CONSEQUENCES COULD BE USEFUL

The economic consequences of a terrorist attack on a tanker could be significant, particularly if one or more ports are closed. Currently, guidance in the Maritime Infrastructure Recovery Plan suggests that ports develop priorities for bringing vessels into port after a closure. Additionally, AMSPs must include a section on crisis management and recovery to ensure the continuity of port operations. At the time of our review, there was no national-level guidance for use by local ports. We identified some ports that, on their own initiative, were incorporating economic recovery considerations into their port-level plans, which could benefit other ports seeking to develop their own plans for mitigating the economic consequences of an attack.

The SAFE Port Act requires the Secretary of Homeland Security to develop protocols for how maritime trade will be reestablished after a terrorist attack. These protocols must include appropriate factors—related to public health, national security, and economic need—that can be used to set priorities for vessels and cargo entering the port after a closure. While the act does not expressly require the development of port-level plans for facilitating the resumption of trade after an incident, DHS could consider developing guidance for ports to use to develop plans for mitigating economic consequences.[72]

PORTS COULD FACE CHALLENGES IN SECURING RESOURCES TO CARRY OUT THEIR RESPONSE PLANS

Ports could face challenges in marshaling resources to improve port response capabilities, including obtaining or sharing needed marine firefighting equipment and training, other training, and interoperable communication systems that allow emergency responders to talk to each other to effectively coordinate their efforts.

Marine Firefighting Equipment and Training

The ports we visited varied considerably in their ability to combat marine fires. Some ports had large fireboats that are designed to deal with fires on tankers, as well as firefighters trained to conduct shipboard firefighting operations. In contrast, other energy commodity ports relied on land-based firefighting companies; these companies told us that they did not have the training and/or the equipment to fight marine fires. See figure 17 for two examples of marine firefighting response.

While some local ports may not be well equipped to handle marine fires, companies operating tankers are required to provide for marine firefighting and salvage capabilities under the Oil Pollution Act of 1990.[73] However, we identified several limitations associated with these requirements:

> *Timeliness of response not spelled out.* OPA 90 does not specify how soon after an event either marine firefighting or salvage must occur. Under a Coast Guard rule proposed in 2002, and not yet issued as final, contracted marine firefighting resources generally would have to be provided within 8 hours after notification of an event, while salvage operations generally would have to begin within 16 hours. Even if this rule were in force, it might not be timely enough to prevent the vessel from sinking.
>
> *Extent of planning for salvage varies widely.* Salvage is important for marine firefighting because a ship may sink from an attack, may be deliberately sunk to control the resulting fire, or may be accidentally sunk by the firefighters because they are not familiar with ship stability issues inherent in the marine firefighting environment. In addition to the OPA 90 requirement, the SAFE Port Act of 2006 requires the development of salvage response plans to supplement Area Maritime Security Plans. While all ACPs for the ports we visited contain sections on salvage, we found that the plans varied widely in

detailing salvage responses. A 2003 National Transportation Safety Board workshop identified potential shortfalls in local salvage planning and/or capabilities as an issue that needed to be addressed.[74] One reason for capability shortfalls identified was that locally available salvage resources may sometimes be lacking.

Source: Coast Guard.

Figure 17. Examples of Marine Firefighting Response.

If ports lack marine firefighting or salvage capabilities, we identified the following other avenues for obtaining resources to enhance these capabilities. However, these avenues carry limitations, mainly related to the speed with which they could be deployed on site.

Mutual aid agreements. Some port community members have mutual aid agreements in place to provide assistance in emergencies. These agreements can be industry-to-industry, municipal-to-municipal, industry-to-municipal, or municipal-to-industry. However, these agreements can have inherent delays in response time if needed resources are located some distance away or require considerable time for redeployment. For example, one refinery noted, in its site emergency manual section for ship fire procedures, that there is a need to evaluate whether refinery responders need to call the local fire department and request fireboat assistance because of a 45-minute delay in subsequent arrival of this resource. If the refinery needs to call for additional assistance from a nearby fire department's fireboats, the delay could be several hours, according to state fire officials.

National Oil Spill Response Resource Inventory. Each Coast Guard Captain of the Port has emergency contracting authority to obtain needed resources. The National Strike Force's Response Resource Inventory lists public and private organizations that can provide these needed spill response resources.[75] The Coast Guard is to review these organizations' resources at least every 3 years to keep an up-to-date resource list. Again, in some cases delay in getting these needed resources to the incident location would occur.

In addition to the differences in the availability of marine firefighting equipment, we found that access to marine firefighting training, which is highly specialized and different from land-based firefighting, can be limited because of distance from a training center or lack of resources. While a range of locations provide firefighter response training for energy commodity fires in the marine environment, these facilities are limited and are sometimes not located near a firefighting response organization that is seeking this training.[76] Some local emergency responders told us they have not received shipboard firefighting training, which is even more specialized than general marine firefighting, and many of the responders we contacted identified the need for additional training. At one port we visited, fire department officials stated that the firefighters had not received this training but would board a burning vessel. See figure 18 for an example of firefighters training to combat an aviation fuel fire.

OTHER TRAINING

We also found differences in training for federally established procedures outlining coordination—known as the incident command system (ICS)—for responding to any incident, including terrorism. Some emergency responders identified a lack of experience and training on this system as a potential concern for effectively coordinating and leading a response to an attack.. The Coast Guard

Source: Coast Guard.

Figure 18. Firefighters Training to Combat an Aviation Fuel Fire.

and fire departments are familiar with ICS because they were using it before September 11, 2001, but law enforcement does not have equivalent experience with it. At the ports we visited, the local Coast Guard and firefighting responders identified themselves as generally compliant with ICS training requirements. Although the FBI would have jurisdictional responsibility for leading the multiagency response to a terrorist attack on a tanker, FBI personnel did not have to comply with ICS training requirements until December 31, 2006.

Interoperable Communications

At the ports we visited, officials identified the lack of fully interoperable communications as an ongoing issue, as did many of the after-action reports we reviewed.[77] Spill and terrorism responders may have difficulty coordinating their emergency response if their communications systems are not interoperable— that is, one agency's equipment may not be able to communicate with another's. For example, according to local emergency planners, during one port exercise in 2006 the responders used their cell phones because of interoperability problems. This workaround may be adequate during an exercise, an FBI official noted, but responders may not be able to rely on the cell phone communications network during an actual event. While interoperability is a problem for emergency responders throughout the nation, responders in the marine environment face additional challenges.[78] These include the need for additional equipment on or near ships so that radio signals can get through to the ship's hold, as well as marine band radios for operating on water.

Response organizations have some options to work around the problem of interoperability. For example, the FBI can use a range of equipment to coordinate the signals of all the various responding agencies' communications equipment, but it takes some time to make this equipment operational because the equipment has to be brought to the site, and each responding organization has to provide a radio to the same location for the workaround system to function. The Coast Guard also has communications equipment for interoperability stored in locations around the nation, but again, there would be a delay in getting this equipment to the site of an incident.

DHS GRANTS MAY BECOME MORE ACCESSIBLE FOR RESPONSE AND RECOVERY PROJECTS, BUT FUNDING DECISIONS REQUIRE BETTER APPLICATION OF PERFORMANCE MEASURES

For ports that may be facing resource shortfalls, finding ways to pay for improvements and enhancements is an issue. One potential funding source is DHS's Port Security Grant Program. In the past, most DHS grants awarded to ports were for terrorism prevention and detection projects (such as fences, cameras, and security systems), rather than for response and recovery projects, according to DHS officials. For some states that contain ports we visited, officials who oversee grant resource distribution also told us that only a limited number of post-incident response project applications, such as marine firefighting assets or shipboard firefighter training, have received grant funding.

This emphasis on prevention and detection is changing. Recent changes in the grant program are more likely to result in consideration of response and recovery projects, according to DHS officials. They told us that the DHS Port Security Grant Program is undergoing a fundamental shift from a facility security focus to a more comprehensive approach to managing risk within ports. The Office of Grants and Training, within the Preparedness Directorate, is working with the Coast Guard to develop an integrated, risk-based decision-making process for allocating grant funds for each port area. This shift in strategy recognizes that port security entails not only prevention and detection activities but also response and recovery capabilities. Plans for fiscal year 2007 grant guidance will place more emphasis on post-incident response projects, according to DHS officials. The SAFE Port Act of 2006 likewise emphasizes a risk-based approach for port security grants.

To make effective judgments about such projects, performance measures are needed to quantitatively determine the spill and terrorism resources that should be available. Such measures help decide the extent to which a given resource is needed to effectively conduct a response within a given time period. At the time of our review, DHS was surveying available emergency response capabilities within a given port, according to officials from DHS's Office of Infrastructure Protection.

In September 2006, the New York City Fire Department Chief of Counterterrorism and Emergency Preparedness questioned whether the nation is prepared for an emergency and called for performance measures that emphasized (1) capability (What can we do?), (2) capacity (How much can we do?), (3) proficiency (How well can we perform?), and (4) deployment (How quickly can we deploy capabilities?). As we have previously reported, in the absence of comparable standards for emergency responder performance, it is difficult to assess whether grant resources will be directed effectively to reduce risk.[79] Without such performance measures, the federal government would not be able to conduct an analysis, based on reducing overall risk, that could be used to set priorities for acquiring needed response resources. Performance measures are critical for setting priorities to effectively allocate federal funds.

The Captain of the Port may assist local authorities in reviewing the adequacy of the port's overall marine firefighting and salvage capability. Such qualitative reviews assess a range of factors related to the nature of operations within the port. However, these assessments cannot set priorities for addressing these shortfalls because they do not have quantitative performance measures that would provide a way to compare one shortfall against another to determine such priorities. Other related assessments face the same priority-setting issues. A recent qualitative advisory report for siting a potential future LNG facility illustrates this problem. The assessment identified the need to send firefighters to specialized fire schools on an annual basis to become trained in fighting LNG fires, as well as to provide local firefighters with additional training on hazardous materials and confined space rescue. The assessment also identified a range of equipment procurement needs, including additional fireboats capable of mitigating a large LNG spill on water as well as dry chemicals and foam caches for extinguishing any resulting fire. While all these shortfalls may need to be addressed, the assessments do not provide a road map for setting federal funding priorities.

In: Maritime Tankers…
Editor: Thomas P. Naylor

ISBN: 978-1-60692-205-7
© 2009 Nova Science Publishers, Inc.

Chapter 6

CONCLUSIONS

The ship-based supply chain for energy commodities remains threatened and vulnerable, and appropriate security throughout the chain is essential to ensure safe and efficient delivery. The threats are especially strong internationally, where the United States faces limitations in ensuring that facilities in foreign ports are meeting security standards and in protecting shipments in international waters. Domestically, the nexus for strengthening security efforts rests with the U.S. Coast Guard, which has primary responsibility for security actions in U.S. ports and waterways. Despite considerable efforts to protect ports and the energy traffic in them, the level of protection is not where the Coast Guard believes it should be. At some ports Coast Guard units are not meeting their own levels of required security activities. Growing demand for Coast Guard resources requires that the Coast Guard take action on several fronts. In adjusting security standards to take into account its limited resources, the Coast Guard needs to assure itself and other stakeholders that its adjustments are based on a careful assessment of risk. This process has begun with the Coast Guard's ongoing assessment of risks associated with all CDC commodities, and since this assessment is already under way, we do not see a need to make a recommendation in this case. The results of that study, and of any comparative analysis that includes hazardous materials not on the CDC list, will be important in a careful and dispassionate analysis for ensuring that available resources are deployed in such a way that commodities receive protection commensurate with the relative risks involved. This is especially important with the expected growth in LNG imports. Similarly, we believe that the results of the risk analyses stemming from use of the Maritime Security Risk Assessment Model will be important in determining how field units can best make use of security resources at their ports. With the ability to compare different targets and different levels of protection offered by security stakeholders, the model should allow the Coast Guard to take a more complete accounting for the various risks at U.S. ports. These two efforts are vital inputs that are needed to ensure an accurate reflection of security risks to tankers and the ports that receive them.

Local Coast Guard units have been active in preparing for the coming growth in LNG shipments, engaging with local law enforcement agencies as a means to augment Coast Guard resources. The assistance the Coast Guard already receives from state and local law enforcement is vital for many units as they try to meet security activity requirements with limited resources. Coast Guard headquarters, however, needs to do more to help these local efforts. More specifically, it needs to begin centralized planning for how to address resource shortfalls across many locations. As LNG facilities continue to multiply, the resulting increase in workload will affect some Coast Guard units but not others, necessitating a centralized response as well as a port-specific one. It is important for the Coast Guard to begin this centralized planning soon, when attention can also be paid to assessing the options for partnering with state or local law enforcement agencies to ensure appropriate security. This broader planning is important for ensuring a proper distribution of resources to best meet the Coast Guard's diverse responsibilities.

In the event of a successful attack on an energy commodity tanker, ports would need to provide an effective, integrated response to protect public safety and the environment, conduct a terrorism investigation, and restore operations in a timely manner. Consequently, clearly defined and understood roles and responsibilities for all stakeholders who would need to respond are needed to ensure an effective response. Operational plans for the response, among the various levels of government involved, should be explicitly linked. As we have reported previously, it is essential that these roles and responsibilities be clearly communicated and understood. Furthermore, while we recognize that ports may have exercise priorities other than responding to a terrorist attack on a tanker, we believe that combined spill and terrorism response exercises should be considered and pursued in ports that are considered to be at risk. In addition, national-level guidance has generally suggested that ports plan for mitigating the economic consequences of an attack. In implementing the post-incident recovery portions of the SAFE Port Act, DHS has an opportunity to provide specific guidance for how ports could plan for lessening potentially significant economic consequences, particularly if an attack results in a port closure. Finally, DHS has just begun to focus more on providing funding for response resources through the Port Security Grant program. However, DHS cannot be assured that it will appropriately target funding to the projects that most reduce overall risk because it has not developed quantitative performance measures. These measures would allow DHS to set priorities for funding on the basis of reducing overall risk. To make effective judgments about such projects, performance measures are needed to quantitatively determine the spill and terrorism resources that should be available.

In: Maritime Tankers…
Editor: Thomas P. Naylor

ISBN: 978-1-60692-205-7
© 2009 Nova Science Publishers, Inc.

Chapter 7

RECOMMENDATIONS FOR EXECUTIVE ACTION

We recommend that the Secretary of Homeland Security direct the Commandant of the Coast Guard to take the following actions:

Develop a national resource allocation plan that will balance the need to meet new LNG security responsibilities with other existing security responsibilities and other Coast Guard missions. This plan needs to encompass goals and objectives, timelines, impacts on other missions, roles of private sector operators, and use of existing state and local agency capacity.

Develop national-level guidance that ports can use to plan for helping to mitigate economic consequences, particularly in the case of port closures.

We also recommend that the Secretary of Homeland Security direct the Commandant of the Coast Guard and that the Attorney General direct the Director of the Federal Bureau of Investigation to work together to take the following two actions:

At the national level, help ensure that a detailed operational plan has been developed that integrates the different spill and terrorism response sections of the National Response Plan.

At the local level, help ensure that spill and terrorism response activities are integrated for the best possible response by maximizing the integration of spill and terrorism response planning and exercises at ports that receive energy commodities where attacks on tankers pose a significant threat.

We recommend that the Secretary of Homeland Security work with federal, state, and local stakeholders to develop explicit performance measures for emergency response capabilities and use them in risk-based analyses to set priorities for acquiring needed response resources.

Chapter 8

AGENCY COMMENTS

We provided a draft of this report to the Departments of Defense, State, Justice, and Homeland Security, including the Coast Guard, for their review and comment. These departments provided formal written comments, except for the Department of State, which provided oral comments. The Department of Defense, in its written comments, concurred with our recommendations. The Departments of Justice, through the FBI, and Homeland Security generally concurred with our recommendations and provided specific comments on the recommendations that are detailed below.

Regarding our recommendation that the Coast Guard develop a national resource allocation plan that takes into account new LNG security responsibilities along with its other mission demands, DHS generally concurred. It stated, however, that while it agrees with the need to address resource demands based on forecasted increases in LNG imports, it also stated that LNG was one of many Certain Dangerous Cargoes that add risk to the maritime environment, and the Coast Guard would address the risk from CDCs as a whole. We agree that there are other dangerous cargoes and it is logical for the Coast Guard to review them holistically in targeting its resources to where the risks are greatest. On the basis of its comments, the Coast Guard plans to examine the risk caused by dangerous commodities, and to take a number of steps to allocate resources. We will monitor the Coast Guard's actions to see if these actions, collectively or in combination with a plan, allow it to optimally allocate its limited resource to meet growing security requirements along with its various other mission needs. Such a plan is important to ensure the best distribution of resources to meet the Coast Guard's diverse responsibilities.

Regarding our recommendation to develop national-level guidance to help ports plan how to mitigate economic consequences, particularly in the case of port closures, DHS generally concurred. It stated that its experience from Hurricane Katrina showed that disruptions to the maritime transportation system can have significant economic impacts and that these impacts need to be considered during recovery actions. It also stated that the Coast Guard, in partnership with CBP, is currently engaged in a broad effort to improve maritime recovery planning. While information on this effort was not provided to us during our review, according to its comment, the Coast Guard seems to recognize the problem and is taking action to address the basis of our concern.

Regarding our recommendation to develop a detailed national operational plan that integrates spill and terrorism sections of the National Response Plan, both DHS and FBI generally concurred. They both stated, however, that the NRP itself already serves as the basis for integrating such response planning, and the FBI did not concur with the need to develop a separate operational plan. As we have noted in prior reports, effective planning and coordination require the development of detailed operational plans for response. While the NRP serves as a strategy-level doctrinal document, it is not an operational plan. We remain concerned that an intentional attack on an energy commodity tanker in a U.S. port may not be met by the best possible response without such a plan to direct the specific circumstance when both the spill and terrorism response sections of the NRP must be integrated and implemented simultaneously. Without a detailed operational plan for this situation, effective and efficient law enforcement investigation and environmental consequence mitigation may be hindered. As we have recently reported, the implementation of the NRP following Hurricane Katrina identified concerns with coordination within and between federal government entities using the NRP. Further, the October 2005 draft version of the MOTR called for DHS and DOJ to develop specific, detailed supporting operational plans for their responsibilities, in close consultation with other departments and agencies. However, this requirement was dropped from the October 2006 final version of the MOTR. As a result, no detailed operational plans exist for the situation described in the response section of this report.[80] We believe our recommendation will help fill the guidance gap between doctrine and port-level operations.

Regarding our recommendation to maximize terrorism and spill response planning and exercises at the local level for the best possible response, DHS generally concurred and FBI concurred. DHS said that while these efforts must be coordinated they need not be an amalgamation. It stated that there are opportunities for this coordination at the local committees that are responsible for planning terrorism and spill response and because the Coast Guard serves as chair for both committees, coordination already occurs. In its comments FBI listed exercises that combined terrorism and spill response. It also stated that local Maritime Liaison Agents were specifically directed to engage agency partners to ensure integration of FBI response. While these actions are beneficial for increased integration, there is no direct link between the actual local terrorism plan and spill response plan. Also, because terrorism response plans have distribution limited to those who need to know, many nonsecurity stakeholders—particularly in the spill response community—would not have access to these plans in an emergency, allowing for the possibility for these stakeholders to take actions that may hinder terrorism response.

Regarding our recommendation that the Secretary of Homeland Security work with federal, state, and local stakeholders to develop explicit performance measures for emergency response capabilities, DHS responded that it was taking the recommendation under advisement and was exploring approaches to address our recommendation. We will follow up with DHS later to get its formal position on this recommendation.

All of the respondents provided technical comments that we incorporated into the report as appropriate. Written comments from DHS are reproduced in appendix V, written comments from FBI are reproduced in appendix VI, and written comments from the Department of Defense are reproduced in appendix VII.

As arranged with your office, unless you publicly announce its contents earlier, we plan on no further distribution of this report until 30 days after its issue date. At that time we will send copies of this report to the Secretary of Homeland Security, the Commandant of the U.S. Coast Guard, and the Attorney General. We will also make copies available to others at no charge at GAO's Web site at http://www.gao.gov.

This report was prepared by two teams within GAO, each of which concentrated on particular aspects of the assignment. If you or your staffs have any questions regarding (1) the types of threats to tankers carrying energy commodities and (2) the measures being taken to protect tankers and the challenges federal agencies face in making these actions effective, please call Stephen L. Caldwell at (202) 512-9610, or caldwells@gao.gov. For questions regarding (1) the potential consequences of a successful attack on tankers or energy infrastructure or (2) the plans in place and the potential challenges in responding to an attack, please call Mark Gaffigan at (202) 512-3841, or gaffiganm@gao.gov. Contact points for our Offices of Congressional Relations and Public Affairs may be found on the last page of this report. Key contributors to this report are listed in appendix IX.

>   Stephen L. Caldwell
>   Director,
>   Homeland Security and Justice Issues
>
>   Mark Gaffigan
>   Acting Director,
>   Natural Resources and Environment Issues

In: Maritime Tankers...
Editor: Thomas P. Naylor

ISBN: 978-1-60692-205-7
© 2009 Nova Science Publishers, Inc.

APPENDIX I: OBJECTIVE, SCOPE, AND METHODOLOGY

The objectives of this report were to (1) determine the types of terrorist threats to tankers carrying energy commodities and the potential consequences of a successful attack; (2) describe what measures are being taken both internationally and domestically to protect these tankers, and what challenges, if any, federal agencies face in making these actions effective; and (3) if a terrorist attack succeeds despite these protective measures, describe what plans are in place to respond and discuss the potential challenges federal agencies may face in responding to a future attack.

To determine the types of terrorist threats to tankers carrying energy commodities, we conducted interviews with maritime intelligence officials from the U.S. Coast Guard and Navy at the National Maritime Intelligence Center.[1] We also met with Coast Guard and Customs and Border Protection officials at headquarters and in the field responsible for port and vessel security to determine their views about maritime terrorism related to energy tankers and infrastructure. During site visits to domestic ports, we also interviewed operators of petroleum waterside facilities and tankers to determine their understanding of the threat environment. We also met with shipping and vessel management companies to discuss their views of the threats they face at foreign loading ports and while in transit to the United States. To gain an international perspective on threats to tankers and loading facilities, we conducted interviews with officials from international maritime organizations, international shipping and petroleum trade associations, vessel operators, vessel insurers, and private security and risk management organizations. We also reviewed classified intelligence documents, including port threat assessments, and government directives related to maritime security.

Continuing with our first objective to describe the potential public safety, environmental, and economic consequences of a successful terrorist attack on a waterside energy facility or tanker, we met with officials from the Department of Energy, the Environmental Protection Agency, the U.S. Maritime Administration, the Coast Guard, and the Federal Energy Regulatory Commission. In addition, we conducted a panel study with academic and industry experts to specifically determine the consequences of an attack on a liquefied natural gas (LNG) tanker. We also visited major petroleum, LNG, and liquefied petroleum gas terminals to discuss possible consequences of attacks at these locations. We also analyzed import data from U.S. government sources for petroleum and other energy commodities into the United States and the ports receiving the imports. Finally, we reviewed published information, such as studies and scholarly articles, to determine the environmental and public health and safety consequences of a terrorist attack to a petroleum waterside facility or tanker.

To describe measures that are being taken to protect these tankers, and what challenges, if any, federal agencies face in making these actions effective, we interviewed a variety of foreign and domestic government officials and private industry representatives. To determine the actions taken in foreign nations, we visited four countries. The selection criteria for our overseas site visits were the amount of energy commodities exported to the United States and the opportunity to learn about maritime anti-terrorism best practices. At the countries we visited we conducted interviews with government officials responsible for maritime security activities and petroleum waterside facility and tanker operators. We also obtained information from the Coast Guard, international maritime organizations, tanker operators, vessel management companies, and insurers to understand port and vessel security practices and procedures overseas and while tankers are in transit to the United States.

To determine the actions taken domestically, we met with officials in the Departments of Homeland Security, Defense, State, Energy, Transportation, and Justice; private sector facility and vessel operators; and state and local officials dealing with homeland security, emergency response, and law enforcement.

We also conducted site visits to a nonprobability sample of petroleum and liquefied gas import and export facilities in the United States. During our site visits we observed security practices and conducted interviews with representatives of federal agencies that oversee the security of the energy facilities, as well as facility security officers and relevant local and state law enforcement officials. The information obtained from these site visits cannot be generalized to all petroleum and liquefied gas import and export facilities nationwide.

We also reviewed government and industry documents and data sources relevant to domestic actions taken by agencies and companies to prevent terrorist attacks. To establish criteria for evaluating the Coast Guard's ability to mitigate the risk of maritime terrorism, we obtained 9 months of Operation Neptune Shield (ONS) Scorecard security performance data—the Coast Guard's performance measurement tool for tracking performance in meeting security activities at the nations most strategically important ports—from select Coast Guard field units covering the months of November 2005 through July 2006. We chose to review scorecard data for ports that the U.S. Maritime Administration identified as being top ports for receiving energy commodity tankers. We calculated the ONS 9-month average of both the monthly activity requirement attainment percentages and share of workload conducted by other government agencies. In conducting this work, we met with Coast Guard headquarters personnel on several occasions to further our understanding. We also asked Coast Guard officials responsible for the scorecard data what steps they took to ensure the reliability of the data and determined that they were sufficiently accurate for our purposes.

To describe what plans are in place for responding to a terrorist attack, should one occur despite protective measures, and discuss the challenges federal agencies may face in responding, we conducted interviews with officials from the Departments of Homeland Security and Justice; the Environmental Protection Agency; as well as officials representing port authorities, state and local offices of public safety and emergency management, oil and gas facilities, and first responders, including police and fire departments. These interviews were conducted to identify spill, terrorism, and economic response plans and priorities; mechanisms for response coordination; access to resources; training availability; types of exercises conducted; potential communications challenges; performance metrics; and information-sharing systems. During our site visits, we observed port operations and the working relationships between some government and private stakeholders. To assess the integration of national and local spill and terrorism response plans, we gathered and reviewed identified plans. Finally, we interviewed emergency response officials and reviewed after-action reports to identify best practices and lessons learned as a result of emergency response exercises and incidents.

We conducted our work from April 2005 to February 2007 in accordance with generally accepted government auditing standards.

Appendix II: Selected Energy Commodities Transported by Tanker into United States

Crude Oil

Crude oil is used to produce a wide array of petroleum products, including gasoline, diesel and jet fuels, heating oil, lubricants, asphalt, plastics, and many other products used for their energy or chemical content.

Crude oils range from very light (high in gasoline) to very heavy (high in residual oils). Sour crude is high in sulfur content. Sweet crude is low in sulfur and therefore often more valuable than other kinds.

Gasoline

A complex mixture of relatively volatile hydrocarbons with or without small quantities of additives, blended to form a fuel suitable for use in spark-ignition engines.

Motor gasoline includes conventional gasoline; all types of oxygenated gasoline, including gasohol; and reformulated gasoline, but excludes aviation gasoline.

JET FUEL

A refined petroleum product used in jet aircraft engines.
Kerosene-type jet fuel is used for commercial and military turbojet and turboprop aircraft engines.
Naphtha-type jet fuel is used primarily for military turbojet and turboprop aircraft engines because it has a lower freeze point than other aviation fuels and meets engine requirements at high altitudes and speeds.

LNG

A natural gas that has been cooled to minus 260 degrees Fahrenheit to a liquid state so that it can be transported.
Consists almost entirely of methane (85-95 percent) along with small concentrations of ethane, propane, butane, and trace amounts of nitrogen.
Mainly used as fuel for electricity generation, home heating, industrial manufacturing, and, to a lesser extent, motor vehicles.

LPG

Group of hydrocarbons, such as propane and butane, derived mainly as a byproduct of oilfield production and crude oil refining processes.
The vast majority of LPG traded internationally consists of propane and butane cargo.
LPG has a variety of agricultural, household, petrochemical, and, to a lesser extent, vehicle fuel applications.

In: Maritime Tankers…
Editor: Thomas P. Naylor

ISBN: 978-1-60692-205-7
© 2009 Nova Science Publishers, Inc.

APPENDIX III: RECENT HIGH-PROFILE TERRORISM INCIDENTS AGAINST TANKERS AND ENERGY INFRASTRUCTURE

Table 4. High-Profile Terrorism Incidents against Tankers and Energy Infrastructure by Target and Attack Method since 2002

Date	Target, location	Attack method	Description
June 2006	Shell Gas Facility, Nigeria	Armed assault	Nigerian militants attacked an energy facility and abducted foreign oil workers in the oil-rich Niger delta. The Movement for the Emancipation of the Niger Delta is responsible for a wave of militant attacks in Nigeria.
Feb. 2006	Saudi Aramco facility, Abqaiq, Saudi Arabia	Suicide attack	Two cars packed with explosives tried to attack a major oil processing facility in Saudi Arabia's eastern province. Al Qaeda suicide attackers were killed along with two Saudi guards.
April 2004	Al Basrah and Khawr Al Amaya oil terminals, Iraq	Suicide attack	Closely timed suicide boat attacks on northern Persian Gulf oil terminals in Iraq left two Navy sailors and one Coast Guardsman dead and five others injured.
Aug. 2003	M/V *Penrider*, en route from Singapore to Malaysia	Armed assault	The Free Aceh Movement claimed responsibility for hijacking the M/V *Penrider*, a fully laden tanker shipping fuel oil in Southeast Asia. Three hostages were eventually released following a ransom payment.

Table 4. (Continued).

Date	Target, location	Attack method	Description
March 2003	Chemical Tanker *Dewi Madrim*, Strait of Malacca	Armed assault	Ten pirates boarded tanker from a speedboat. Pirates took the helm, altered the speed, disabled ship's radio, and steered the vessel for an hour. Pirates left with cash and abducted captain and first officer.
Oct. 2002	M/V *Limburg*, Yemen	Suicide attack	Small boat filled with explosives rammed the side of the French-flagged oil tanker *Limburg* as it was approaching the Ash Shihr Terminal several miles off the coast of Yemen. The suicide attack killed one crew member and 90,000 barrels of oil spilled.

Source: GAO.

In: Maritime Tankers…
Editor: Thomas P. Naylor

ISBN: 978-1-60692-205-7
© 2009 Nova Science Publishers, Inc.

APPENDIX IV:
ASSESSING AND MANAGING RISKS
USING A RISK MANAGEMENT APPROACH

Risk management is a systematic approach for analyzing risk and deciding how best to address it. Because resources are limited and cannot eliminate all risks, careful choices need to be made in deciding which actions yield the greatest benefit. Figure 19 depicts a risk management framework that is our synthesis of government requirements and prevailing best practices previously reported.[1] To be effective, this process must be repeated when threats or conditions change to incorporate any new information to adjust and revise the assessments and actions.

Setting strategic goals, objectives, and constraints is a key first step in implementing a risk management approach and helps to ensure that management decisions are focused on achieving a strategic purpose. These decisions should take place in the context of an agency's strategic plan that includes goals and objectives that are clear, concise, and measurable.

Risk assessment, a critical step in the approach, helps decision makers identify and evaluate potential risks so that countermeasures can be designed and implemented to prevent or mitigate the effects of risk. Risk assessment is a qualitative and/or quantitative determination of the likelihood of an adverse event occurring and the severity, or impact, of its consequences. Risk assessment in a homeland security application often involves assessing three key elements—threat, criticality, and vulnerability:

A threat assessment identifies and evaluates potential threats on the basis of factors such as capabilities, intentions, and past activities.

A criticality or consequence assessment evaluates and prioritizes assets and functions in terms of specific criteria, such as their importance to public safety and the economy, as a basis for identifying which structures or processes are relatively more important to protect from attack.

A vulnerability assessment identifies weaknesses that may be exploited by identified threats and suggests options to address those weaknesses.

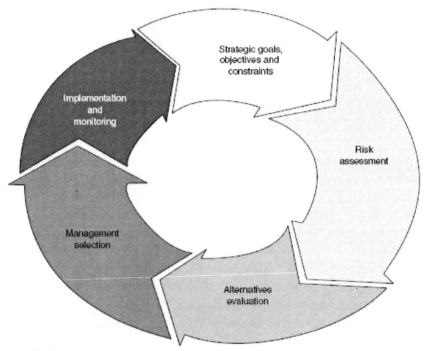

Source: GAO.

Figure 19. Risk Management Framework.

Information from these three assessments contributes to an overall risk assessment that characterizes risks on a scale such as high, medium, or low and provides input for evaluating alternatives and management prioritization of security initiatives.

The next two steps involve deciding what mitigation measures to adopt. Alternatives evaluation considers what actions may be needed to address identified risks, the associated costs of taking these actions, and any resulting benefits. This information is provided to agency management to aid in completing the next step—selecting alternative actions best suited to the unique needs of the organization.

The final step in the approach involves implementing the selected actions and evaluating the extent to which they mitigate risk. This involves developing criteria for monitoring the performance of these actions and follow-up to ensure that these actions are effective and reflect evolving risk.

Risk management has received widespread support from Congress, the President, and the Secretary of Homeland Security as a tool that can help set priorities and inform decisions about mitigating risks.

REFERENCES

[1] In this report, the term "energy commodities" refers to crude oil, refined petroleum products, and natural gas.
[2] While most petroleum is imported as crude oil and refined in U.S. terminals, tankers also import products already refined from crude oil. Crude oil is refined into petroleum products using several processes that start with simple distillation. The products are referred to as "light" petroleum products (the group of petroleum products with lower boiling temperatures, including gasoline, jet fuel, and diesel fuel) and "heavy" petroleum products (those that remain after the lighter products are distilled away, such as asphalt). See appendix II for a description of assorted energy commodities imported into the United States by tanker.
[3] LNG is primarily methane, while LPG is propane or butane that has been cooled or pressurized to reduce its volume. LPG imports are relatively small in volume compared to LNG imports.
[4] Canada is the other primary supplier of crude oil and natural gas to the United States, but its exports arrive by pipeline.
[5] The five are located at Everett, Massachusetts (near Boston); Cove Point, Maryland (on Chesapeake Bay); Elba Island, Georgia (near Savannah); Lake Charles, Louisiana (in western Louisiana); and offshore in the Gulf of Mexico, 116 miles south of the Louisiana coast.
[6] In addition to the 11 onshore LNG terminals, 2 offshore terminals have been approved by the Maritime Administration, which is responsible for approving new offshore LNG facilities. A total of 32 new onshore and offshore LNG facilities have been proposed or approved by either the Federal Energy Regulatory Commission or the Maritime Administration.

[7] IMO is an agency of the United Nations that facilitates international regulation of safety and security of commercial shipping.

[8] Countries where ports are located are referred to as "port states." Countries where ships are registered are referred to as "flag states." As of November 30, 2006, there were 156 contracting governments to the SOLAS Convention, representing 99 percent of the world shipping fleet by tonnage.

[9] Pub. L. No. 107-295, 116 Stat. 2064.

[10] Pub. L. No. 101-380, 104 Stat. 484.

[11] See: GAO, Maritime Transportation: Major Oil Spills Occur Infrequently, but Risks to the Federal Oil Spill Fund Remain, GAO-07-1085 (Washington, D.C.: Sept. 7, 2007).

[12] In general, the scope of our review is limited to terrorist attacks. We did not evaluate the security of the maritime energy supply chain from other attacks, such as the militaries of other countries, or from natural disasters, such as hurricanes or earthquakes. For information on ports and natural disasters see GAO, *Port Risk Management: Additional Federal Guidance Would Aid Ports in Disaster Planning and Recovery*, GAO-07-412 (Washington, D.C.: Mar. 28, 2007), and GAO, *Coast Guard: Observations on the Preparation, Response, and Recovery Missions Related to Hurricane Katrina*, GAO-06-903 (Washington, D.C.: July 31, 2006).

[13] Nonprobability sampling is a method of sampling where observations are selected in a manner that is not completely random, usually using specific characteristics of the population as criteria. Results from nonprobability samples cannot be used to make inferences about a population because in a nonprobability sample, some elements of the population being studied have no chance or an unknown chance of being selected as part of the sample.

[14] We have also reported the views of our findings related specifically to LNG in a separate report. See GAO, Maritime Security: Public Safety Consequences of a Terrorist Attack on a Tanker Carrying Liquefied Natural Gas Need Clarification, GAO-07-316 (Washington, D.C.: Feb. 22, 2007).

[15] Specific details regarding the operationalization and integration of spill and terrorism response plans were provided in the Sensitive Security Information version of this report.

[16] A barrel is equivalent to 42 gallons of oil.

[17] The Ultra Large Crude Carrier type of tanker is even larger than the Very Large Crude Carrier, but because of changing route economics, Ultra Large Crude Carriers make up a small portion of the overall tanker market.

[18] LOOP, the only U.S. deepwater oil port that can handle fully loaded Very Large Crude Carriers, is located 18 miles off the Louisiana coast and currently handles about 10 percent of U.S. crude oil imports.
[19] The U.S. Maritime Administration reports that in 2005, 79 percent of tanker calls (U.S.-flag and foreign-flag) at U.S. ports were by double-hull tankers.
[20] This includes both crude oil and petroleum products.
[21] Imports of natural gas from Mexico also arrive in the United States via pipeline.
[22] This section presents petroleum and LNG import data for 2004. Although 2005 data are more recent, normal petroleum import patterns were disrupted by the series of hurricanes that affected the Gulf Coast. Because of these impacts, 2004 data are more representative.
[23] The National Strategy for Maritime Security (Washington, D.C.: Sept. 2005).
[24] See GAO, Maritime Security: Enhancements Made, but Implementation and Sustainability Remain Key Challenges, GAO-05-448T (Washington, D.C.: May 2005).
[25] See appendix V for additional information on risk management.
[26] For further discussion of risk management as it relates to homeland security, see GAO, Risk Management: Further Refinements Needed to Assess Risks and Prioritize Protective Measures at Ports and Other Critical Infrastructure, GAO-06-91 (Washington, D.C.: December. 2005).
[27] See appendix III for descriptions of recent terrorist attacks against maritime or energy targets.
[28] MARSEC is a three-tiered system developed by the Coast Guard to communicate the prevailing threat environment to the marine elements of the national transportation system, including ports, facilities, and critical assets and infrastructure. The levels align closely with DHS's color-coded Homeland Security Alert System in the following way: MARSEC 1 applies when threat conditions Green, Blue, or Yellow are set; MARSEC 2 applies when threat condition Orange is set; and MARSEC 3 applies when threat condition Red is set.
[29] Pub. L. No. 109-347, 120 Stat. 1884.
[30] Michael D. Greenberg et al., *Maritime Terrorism: Risk and Liability* (Washington, D.C.: RAND Corporation, 2006), 22.
[31] Piracy is defined by the International Maritime Bureau, a division of the International Chamber of Commerce that tracks and reports pirate attacks, as, "an act of boarding or attempting to board any ship with the apparent

intent to commit theft or any other crime and with the apparent intent or capability to use force in the furtherance of that act."

[32] Coast Guard Mission Capabilities: Hearing before the Subcommittee on Coast Guard and Maritime Transportation of the House Committee on Transportation and Infrastructure, 109th Cong. 18-25 (2006) (statement of Rear Admiral Wayne Justice and Rear Admiral Joseph Nimmich, U.S. Coast Guard, Department of Homeland Security).

[33] There are three types of LPG tankers: fully refrigerated, partially refrigerated, and fully pressurized, which describes the method used to keep the LPG cargo in a liquid state. Partially refrigerated LPG tankers keep their cargo in a liquid state with a combination of refrigeration and pressure. Generally larger LPG tankers, like those used in international trade, are fully refrigerated.

[34] Data are from National Research Council of the National Academies. "Oil in the Sea III: Inputs, Fates, and Effects" the National Academies Press: Washington, D.C. 2003. Numbers do not add to 100 percent due to rounding.

[35] As we will discuss later in this report, however, concerns about supply disruption can have an effect on price, and in the case of the *Exxon Valdez* spill, price was temporarily affected.

[36] Lightering is the process of transferring oil at sea from a very large or ultra-large carrier to smaller tankers that are capable of entering the port.

[37] Partick L .Anderson. "Lost Earnings Due to the West Coast Port Shutdown—Preliminary Estimate--Anderson Economic Group LLC (Lansing, Michigan, Oct. 7, 2002).

[38] The estimate is lower than some other studies that examined the incident because it took into consideration that cargoes were simply delayed, and not lost entirely.

[39] Peter Gordon; James Moore II; Harry Richardson; and Pan Qisheng, "The Economic Impact of a Terrorist Attack on the Twin Ports of Los Angeles-Long Beach" in *The Economic Impacts of Terrorist Attacks*, Peter Gordon, James Moore II, and Harry Richardson, eds., (Northampton, Massachusetts, 2006).

[40] John S. Cook and Charles P. Shirkey. "A Review of Valdez Oil Spill Market Impacts," *Petroleum Marketing Monthly*, a publication of the Energy Information Administration, March 1989.

[41] Crew list visas are nonimmigrant visas that cover all crew members of a vessel or aircraft included on a master list submitted to State Department officials.

[42] See GAO, Border Security: Strengthened Visa Process Would Benefit from Additional Management Actions by State and DHS, GAO-05-859 (Washington D.C.: Sept. 13, 2005).

[43] The Navy and Coast Guard also work with foreign nations to improve their ability to prevent terrorist attacks in the waters around their countries. In exercises such as South East Asia Cooperation Against Terrorism (SEACAT) and Cooperation Afloat Readiness and Training (CARAT), the Navy works to improve other countries' skills and to increase interoperability among nations. In these exercises the forces from the different countries practice boarding tactics and techniques and other skills. The Navy and Coast Guard also take part in multinational conferences, such as the Alameda Conference on East Asian and Pacific Region Maritime Security in February 2006. This conference, sponsored by the Coast Guard, was aimed at coordinating maritime security assistance for the Strait of Malacca region and beyond. Another conference, held in Benin and sponsored by the Navy, was aimed at improving security around the Gulf of Guinea.

[44] The Coast Guard has contracted with a satellite communication provider to test the ability to receive signals up to 2000 miles from U.S. shores.

[45] Since September 11, 2001, the funding for the Coast Guard's homeland security mission area—which consists of ports, waterways, and coastal security; illegal drug interdiction; undocumented migrant interdiction; defense readiness; and other law enforcement—has increased substantially. It now roughly equals funding for all Coast Guard non-homeland security mission programs. For example, in the Coast Guard's fiscal year 2007 budget request, Coast Guard requested a total of $8.4 billion, of which $4.5 billion (54 percent) was requested for Coast Guard maritime homeland security missions. The Coast Guard does not separate funding for security activities to protect energy commodity tankers.

[46] Coast Guard conducts various actions to ensure facility and vessel operators are complying with MTSA. The Coast Guard conducts annual site visits and spot checks to ensure facility operators are complying with their MTSA-approved security plan—plans for access control, physical security, and perimeter surveillance. In ensuring vessel operator MTSA compliance, the Coast Guard conducts, among other activities, boardings to ensure that the crew have appropriate documentation or that the vessel, when moored, is taking steps to restrict access. Furthermore, should the Coast Guard identify security-related deficiencies by vessel or facility operators, it will increase the frequency of its spot inspections until it determines that the vessel or facility operators have taken the necessary corrective actions. We currently

have another assignment under way examining compliance with MTSA requirements in more detail. As a result, we do not address MTSA compliance in detail in this report.

[47] CBP and the Coast Guard work together to handle high risk crew members and to ensure that those crewmembers do not leave the tanker. They require actions such as posting guards to prevent unauthorized personnel from leaving the vessel and visits to the ship by agency personnel to ensure high risk personnel are still on board.

[48] CDCs are defined in 33 C.F.R. § 160.204, a section of Coast Guard regulations that addresses ports and waterways safety. The list primarily includes nonenergy products that are flammable, toxic, or explosive, such as chlorine and sulfur dioxide.

[49] The guidance is contained in a Coast Guard operations order called Operation Neptune Shield (ONS). First issued in 2003 and revised periodically since, it contains a classified set of requirements establishing the Coast Guard's homeland security activity levels. As such, the order sets scalable performance minimums that escalate as the MARSEC level increases.

[50] In addition to state and local law enforcement support, the Department of Defense (Defense) can also support Coast Guard maritime homeland security operations based on memorandums of agreement between Defense and the Department of Homeland Security. Examples of military support provided to the Coast Guard by Defense include conducting mine countermeasures in ports, surveillance of terrorist maritime movements, and sustaining Defense and Coast Guard personnel and platforms conducting offshore operations for extended periods of time. According to a departmental official, Defense has not been asked to provide these capabilities in a domestic maritime terrorism incident involving tankers or energy infrastructure to date.

[51] Area Maritime Security Committees were required by Coast Guard regulations implementing MTSA and are composed of the local Coast Guard Captain of the Port and officials of federal, local, and state governments; law enforcement agencies; maritime industry and labor organizations; and other port stakeholders that may be affected by security policies. The responsibilities of the committees include, in part, identifying critical port infrastructure, identifying risks to the port, developing mitigation strategies for these risks, and communicating appropriate security information to port stakeholders.

[52] See GAO, Risk Management: Further Refinement Needed to Assess Risks and Prioritize Protective Measures at Ports and Other Critical Infrastructure, GAO-06-91 (Washington, D.C.: Dec. 15, 2005).
[53] Coast Guard policy requires Coast Guard field units to conduct additional security activities at higher MARSEC levels.
[54] The objective of a consequence analysis for CDC commodities is to predict the blast loads, damage to nearby structures, ship integrity, heat load, potential mass casualties, environmental hazards, and potential disruption to both commercial and military operations.
[55] The Maritime Security Risk Assessment Model is a tool developed by the Coast Guard to determine relative risks at ports that can be compared both within the port and among ports.
[56] An existing LNG import facility is located in Puerto Rico.
[57] Pub. L. No. 109-58, 119 Stat. 594.
[58] Preexisting interagency plans are incorporated into sections of the NRP as supporting operational plans. The National Oil and Hazardous Substances Pollution Contingency Plan (NCP) is the subplan that serves as the basis for federal spill response activities under the NRP section for spill response (Emergency Support Function #10).
[59] 6 U.S.C. § 942.
[60] MTSA calls for plans "to deter and minimize damage from transportation security incidents," such as terrorist attacks. For the purposes of this report the phrases "terrorism response plans" and "terrorism response" are substituted.
[61] GAO, Catastrophic Disasters: Enhanced Leadership, Capabilities, and Accountability Controls Will Improve the Effectiveness of the Nation's Preparedness, Response, and Recovery System, GAO-06-618 (Washington, D.C.: Sept. 6, 2006).
[62] USCG headquarters officials reported that, since the end of GAO's audit work, the USCG and the FBI have jointly responded in two maritime cases that reflected a nexus between environmental response and transnational crime/terrorism: M/V *Tong Chang* and M/V *Dubai Express*. GAO was not able to review these cases and cannot comment on them because they occurred after audit work completion. In addition, USCG headquarters officials stated that, at the direction of the President, DHS, DOJ and DOD completed the Maritime Operational Threat Response Forces (MOTR Forces) plan, in July 2007. According to USCG headquarters officials, the MOTR Forces plan is a supporting plan to the base MOTR, designed to permit the interoperability and synchronization of DHS, DOJ, and DOD

maritime competencies and capabilities. GAO was not able to review and cannot comment on the MOTR Forces support plan because it was developed after audit work completion.

[63] GAO-06-618.
[64] Specific details regarding exercising spill and terrorism response plans were provided in the Sensitive Security Information version of this report.
[65] The U.S. Coast Guard SONS exercise program is designed to increase the preparedness of the entire response organization from the field level to agency heads in Washington, D.C. This program is focused on exercising the entire National Response System at the local, regional, and national levels using large-scale, high-probability oil and hazardous material incidents that result from unintentional causes such as maritime casualties and natural disasters.
[66] U.S. Department of Justice, Office of the Inspector General, *The Federal Bureau of Investigation's Efforts to Protect the Nation's Seaports*, Audit Report 06-26 (Washington, D.C.: March 2006).
[67] Specific details regarding coordination of the MOTR were provided in the Sensitive Security Information version of this report.
[68] Following the September 11, 2001, terrorist attacks, Environmental Protection Agency (EPA) guidance recognized that local emergency spill planning committees should consider the possibility of terrorist events as they review existing plans and consider how to incorporate counterterrorism measures. This guidance noted that one difference in dealing with a terrorist-derived incident is that law enforcement officials will be involved in the response as investigators, and that their priorities may create emergency response coordination challenges that spill response committees should address in their plan.
[69] According to FBI officials, FBI policy is that every field office of the FBI that has within its jurisdiction a port or other navigable waterway will have an agent who is assigned to serve in the MLA position. FBI officials stated that there are 124 MLAs around the country for all navigable waterways and ports where field offices are located.
[70] Coast Guard headquarters is reviewing the MTR for possible dissemination as a model approach to coordinating a terrorism response.
[71] Testimony of the Honorable Michael P. Jackson, Deputy Secretary, Department of Homeland Security, before the U.S. House of Representative Committee on Homeland Security on H. R. 4954 (To improve maritime and cargo security through enhanced layered defenses, and for other purposes), April 4, 2006.

[72] Specific details regarding the operationalization and integration of spill and terrorism response plans were provided in the Sensitive Security Information version of this report.

[73] As implemented by Coast Guard regulations in 33 § CFR 155.1050(k).

[74] "Marine Salvage Capabilities Responding to Terrorist Attacks in U.S. Ports—Actions to Improve Readiness," Report of the Committee for Marine Salvage Response Capability: A Workshop of the National Transportation Safety Board, August 5–6, 2003, Washington, D.C.

[75] The National Strike Force was established in 1973. Originally composed of three 17-member Strike Teams, today's National Strike Force totals over 200 active duty, civilian, and reserve Coast Guard personnel and includes the National Strike Force Coordination Center (NSFCC), the Atlantic Strike Team, the Gulf Strike Team, the Pacific Strike Team, and the Public Information Assist Team located at the NSFCC. NSFCC provides support and standardization guidance to the Atlantic, Gulf, and Pacific strike teams. NSFCC is also home to National Response Resources Inventory and the National Oil Spill Removal Organization Classification Program.

[76] This training is necessary for responding to an attack on a tanker, because marine firefighting presents special considerations that are not present in land-based firefighting, such as vessel stability, water discharge discipline, vessel dewatering, and shipboard firefighting systems (such as onboard firefighting foam deluge systems). The National Fire Protection Association developed NFPA 1405: "Guide for Land-Based Firefighters Who Respond to Marine Vessels" at the request of, and in cooperation with, the Coast Guard and with the assistance of the fire service and maritime communities in response to a recognized need in this area for firefighter training.

[77] The DHS fiscal 2007 appropriations act calls for DHS to conduct baseline interoperability assessments across the country by October 2007, and every 5 years thereafter.

[78] GAO, Homeland Security: Federal Leadership and Intergovernmental Cooperation Required to Achieve First Responder Interoperable Communications, GAO-04-740 (Washington, D.C.: July 20, 2004).

[79] GAO, Homeland Security – DHS' Efforts to Enhance First Responders' All-Hazards Capabilities Continue to Evolve, GAO-05-652 (Washington, D.C.: July 20005).

[80] USCG headquarters officials stated that, at the direction of the President, DHS, DOJ, and DOD completed the Maritime Operational Threat Response Forces plan, in July 2007. According to USCG headquarters officials, the MOTR Forces plan is a supporting plan to the base MOTR, designed to

permit the interoperability and synchronization of DHS, DOJ, and DOD maritime competencies and capabilities. GAO was not able to review and cannot comment on the MOTR Forces support plan because it was developed after audit work completion.

APENDIX I

[1] Central Intelligence Agency officials declined our request for a briefing on threats to energy tankers.

APPENDIX IV

[1] See GAO, Risk Management: Further Refinements Needed to Assess Risks and Prioritize Protective Measures at Ports and Other Critical Infrastructure, GAO-06-91 (Washington, D.C.: December 2005).

INDEX

9

9/11, 5, 23
9/11 Commission, 5, 23

A

academic, 6, 88
access, 4, 15, 22, 37, 40, 41, 48, 61, 66, 71, 85, 89, 103
accidental, 5
accidents, 21
accounting, 78
accuracy, 29, 35, 40
acrylonitrile, 49
activity level, 104
additives, 91
adverse event, 95
Africa, 16, 44
agent, 66, 106
agents, 65
agricultural, 92
aid, 71, 96
air, 22, 23
Al Qaeda, 28, 93
Alaskan North Slope, 34, 37
Algeria, 3, 18
alternative, 97
alternatives, 36, 96

ammonia, 49
ammonium, 49
analysts, 51
Angola, 18
animals, 33
anti-terrorism, 8, 41, 88
appendix, 85, 86, 99, 101
application, 4, 95
apprehending suspects, 61
appropriations, 107
Arabia, 3, 18, 28, 31, 93
Asia, 22, 31, 93, 103
Asian, 103
asphalt, 91, 99
assault, 7, 25, 28, 93, 94
assaults, 29, 30
assessment, 50, 75, 77, 95, 96
assets, 53, 74, 96, 101
assignment, 85, 104
Atlantic, 4, 22, 53, 107
Atlantic Ocean, 22
atmosphere, 32
attacker, 27
attacks, vii, 4, 5, 7, 8, 10, 14, 21, 22, 23, 25, 26, 27, 28, 29, 30, 31, 37, 39, 45, 50, 57, 61, 63, 82, 88, 89, 93, 100, 101, 103, 105, 106
Attorney General, 10, 81, 85
auditing, 6, 89
authority, 4, 5, 14, 17, 26, 71
availability, 35, 46, 49, 71, 89

B

background information, 43
Bahrain, 31
benchmark, 41
benefits, 96
birds, 34
Black Sea, 22
boats, 7, 10, 42, 52, 53
boiling, 1, 32, 99
bomb, 37
Boston, 36, 99
Bureau of Consular Affairs, 15
burn, 32, 33, 34
burning, 61, 72
burns, 32
butane, 92, 99

C

Canada, 16, 18, 43, 99
capacity, 36, 48, 49, 53, 74, 81
cargo, 1, 6, 8, 13, 15, 16, 20, 22, 29, 31, 35, 46, 47, 59, 61, 68, 92, 102, 106
Caribbean, 16
carrier, 16, 102
CDC, 1, 46, 47, 49, 50, 77, 105
cell, 73
cell phones, 73
Central Intelligence Agency, 108
centralized, 78
channels, 20, 22, 59
chemical content, 91
chemicals, 5, 61, 75
China, 22
chloride, 49
chlorine, 49, 104
civilian, 107
clams, 33
cleanup, 6, 33, 35, 65, 66
closure, 33, 35, 36, 37, 38, 68, 78
Co, 103, 107
Coast Guard, 2, 5, 6, 8, 9, 13, 14, 15, 17, 25, 26, 27, 30, 31, 35, 39, 41, 42, 43, 44, 45, 46, 47, 48, 49, 50, 51, 52, 53, 54, 56, 57, 58, 61, 63, 64, 65, 66, 68, 69, 70, 71, 72, 73, 74, 77, 78, 81, 83, 84, 85, 87, 88, 89, 93, 100, 101, 102, 103, 104, 105, 106, 107
coastal areas, 22
collisions, 7, 25
commerce, 30
Committee on Homeland Security, 2, 106
commodity, 7, 8, 9, 20, 23, 25, 31, 34, 36, 39, 43, 45, 46, 48, 57, 60, 61, 62, 63, 69, 71, 78, 84, 89, 103
communication, 66, 69, 103
communication systems, 69
communities, 62, 64, 66, 107
community, 71, 85
compensation, 5
complexity, 30
compliance, 8, 14, 15, 17, 40, 41; 48, 103
confidence, 35
conflict, 29
Congress, iv, 5, 7, 23, 25, 26, 54, 67, 97
conspiracy, 30
constraints, 36, 49, 95
construction, 4, 5, 53
consumers, 8, 37
consumption, 18, 34, 35
contamination, 61
contingency, 5, 58
continuity, 59, 68
control, 17, 29, 30, 40, 48, 61, 69, 103
cooling, 3, 32
coordination, 5, 10, 21, 57, 58, 63, 64, 65, 66, 67, 72, 84, 89, 106
Coping, 45
corporations, 5
cost-effective, 5
costs, 8, 35, 37, 52, 96
cost-sharing, 52
countermeasures, 95, 104
counterterrorism, 106
covering, 89
crime, 56, 61, 65, 67, 102, 105
crisis management, 68
critical assets, 101

critical infrastructure, 5, 30, 46, 48
crude oil, vii, 3, 16, 18, 20, 32, 33, 34, 35, 36, 47, 92, 99, 101
cryogenic, 32
CSF, 1, 66
customers, 36
Customs and Border Protection, 1, 6, 8, 15, 87
Customs and Border Protection (CBP), 8, 15

D

danger, 8, 32, 33, 43, 46
database, 14, 40, 41, 43
deaths, 66
decision makers, 54, 95
decision-making process, 8, 37, 55, 74
decisions, 5, 23, 48, 51, 54, 95, 97
defense, 103
defenses, 106
definition, 20
Delaware, 34, 35
delivery, 77
demand, 4, 34, 38, 52, 77
Department of Defense, 1, 15, 57, 83, 85, 104
Department of Energy, 34, 38, 88
Department of Homeland Security, 1, 5, 15, 26, 102, 104, 106
Department of Justice, 1, 15, 58, 65, 106
Department of State, 15, 83
desire, 7
detection, 73, 74
diesel, 3, 33, 91, 99
diesel fuel, 99
direct action, 42
direct costs, 35
directives, 88
disabled, 30, 94
disaster, 66
discipline, 107
disseminate, 15
distillation, 99
distribution, 74, 78, 83, 85

division, 14, 101
draft, 16, 83, 84
drug interdiction, 103
drug smuggling, 25
drugs, 31
duration, 35
duties, 54

E

East Asia, 103
ecological, 35
economic welfare, 8
economics, 100
Egypt, 18
electricity, 92
emergency management, 5, 66, 89
emergency preparedness, 58
emergency response, 6, 10, 65, 67, 73, 74, 82, 85, 88, 89, 106
employees, 26
employment, 37
Energy Information Administration, 3, 18, 19, 20, 21, 22, 102
Energy Policy Act, 52
Energy Policy Act of 2005, 52
energy supply, 5, 8, 20, 21, 29, 35, 100
engines, 91, 92
England, 36
environment, 5, 8, 17, 20, 25, 32, 33, 61, 70, 71, 73, 78, 83, 87, 101
environmental effects, 32
environmental impact, 25, 31, 33
Environmental Protection Agency, 1, 6, 88, 89, 106
EPA, 1, 106
equipment, 30, 52, 55, 64, 69, 71, 73, 75
ethane, 92
Europe, 16
evaporation, 16
exercise, 64, 65, 66, 67, 73, 78, 106
expansions, 51
expert, iv
expertise, 50
explosions, 31, 32, 33, 64

explosives, 27, 28, 93, 94
exports, 99
exposure, 22
Exxon, 5, 33, 34, 35, 37, 102
Exxon Valdez, 5, 33, 34, 35, 37, 102

F

FBI, 1, 5, 6, 9, 15, 56, 57, 58, 61, 63, 64, 65, 66, 68, 72, 73, 83, 84, 85, 105, 106
fears, 8, 31, 38
February, 6, 28, 89, 103
Federal Bureau of Investigation, 1, 5, 15, 81, 106
Federal Energy Regulatory Commission, 4, 6, 51, 88, 99
federal funds, 74
federal government, 4, 10, 58, 64, 74, 84
federal grants, 52, 55
federal law, 53, 57
Federal Register, 35
feet, 3, 16, 19
fencing, 48
financial resources, 52
financial support, 9
fire, 5, 7, 9, 25, 29, 31, 32, 33, 34, 43, 59, 61, 69, 71, 72, 75, 89, 107
fires, 10, 32, 33, 34, 69, 71, 75
firms, 37
first responders, 5, 61, 89
fish, 33
fishing, 33
flame, 32, 33
flexibility, 49
flow, 13, 21, 22, 37, 59
foreign nation, 88, 103
France, 43
freedom, 22
frostbite, 32
FSP, 58
fuel, vii, 3, 20, 32, 33, 49, 50, 52, 72, 91, 92, 93, 99
funding, 5, 10, 26, 50, 52, 53, 54, 73, 75, 78, 103
funds, 10, 55, 74

G

GAO, vii, 7, 14, 15, 18, 20, 21, 22, 47, 51, 56, 58, 60, 62, 67, 85, 94, 96, 100, 101, 103, 105, 106, 107, 108
gas, 1, 3, 4, 5, 6, 16, 18, 20, 30, 32, 36, 49, 63, 88, 89, 92, 99, 101
gases, vii, 3, 5, 9, 32
gasoline, 3, 20, 33, 35, 37, 47, 50, 91, 99
generation, 92
generators, 36
geography, 20
Georgia, 99
Germany, 43
global supply chain, 3, 16
goals, 66, 67, 81, 95
government, 3, 4, 5, 6, 8, 10, 13, 14, 15, 17, 26, 29, 35, 39, 40, 44, 52, 58, 64, 74, 78, 84, 88, 89, 95, 100, 104
grants, 10, 27, 52, 53, 55, 73, 74
grounding, 17
groups, 5, 23, 29, 30, 57, 59
growth, 77, 78
guidance, 6, 10, 41, 43, 46, 48, 49, 57, 58, 59, 65, 66, 68, 69, 74, 78, 81, 84, 104, 106, 107
Guinea, 29, 103
Gulf Coast, 20, 101
Gulf of Mexico, 36, 99
Gulf of Oman, 21, 43, 44

H

handling, 16
harm, 32, 33
hazardous materials, 57, 59, 61, 63, 64, 75, 77
hazardous substance, 58
hazards, 105
health, 51, 59, 68, 88
heat, 32, 105
heating, 3, 33, 36, 91, 92
heating oil, 3, 33, 91
helicopters, 53

Index

high-risk, 65, 104
hip, 94
hips, 20, 29, 61
home heating oil, 33
homeland security, 1, 2, 5, 6, 10, 15, 23, 26, 31, 45, 54, 59, 64, 68, 81, 82, 83, 85, 86, 88, 89, 95, 97, 101, 102, 103, 104, 106, 107
host, 5, 8, 39, 41
House, 2, 68, 102, 106
household, 92
human, 27, 31, 47, 51
Hurricane Katrina, 63, 64, 84, 100
hurricanes, 100, 101
hydro, 91, 92
hydrocarbons, 91, 92
hypothermia, 34

I

identification, 40, 44, 48, 63
identity, 44
immigrants, 31
immigration, 43
implementation, 40, 41, 58, 59, 64, 84
imports, vii, 3, 16, 18, 20, 21, 34, 36, 77, 83, 88, 99, 101
in situ, 30
Incidents, vi, 93
income, 37
Indian, 21, 43, 44
Indian Ocean, 21, 43, 44
indirect effect, 37
Indonesia, 22, 43
industrial, 37, 92
industry, 6, 16, 30, 39, 41, 51, 71, 88, 89, 104
inferences, 100
infinite, 35
information sharing, 15
infrastructure, 5, 22, 26, 27, 29, 30, 32, 33, 46, 48, 53, 59, 66, 85, 87, 101, 104
injuries, 66
injury, iv
inspections, 103

Inspector General, 65, 106
instability, 22
insurance, 14
integration, 10, 65, 66, 81, 85, 89, 100, 107
integrity, 105
intelligence, 7, 15, 25, 26, 27, 29, 30, 31, 40, 57, 87
intentions, 27, 95
interaction, 65, 68
International Chamber of Commerce, 14, 101
international standards, 14
international trade, 102
interoperability, 73, 103, 105, 107, 108
interviews, 6, 87, 88, 89
Investigations, 61
investigative, 57
Iraq, 4, 18, 27, 42, 93
Italy, 43

J

January, 50, 54
Japan, 41
jet fuel, vii, 3, 20, 33, 50, 91, 92, 99
Jordanian, 29
judgment, 50
jurisdiction, 17, 40, 106

K

Katrina, 63, 64, 84, 100
kidnapping, 29
killing, 27
King, 2

L

labor, 37, 104
land, 4, 15, 22, 28, 69, 71, 107
large-scale, 106
law, 6, 8, 14, 26, 39, 46, 47, 52, 53, 57, 61, 66, 72, 78, 84, 88, 103, 104, 106

law enforcement, 6, 8, 14, 39, 46, 47, 52, 53, 57, 61, 66, 72, 78, 84, 88, 103, 104, 106
laws, 17
lead, 13, 15, 45, 57
leadership, 10
licensing, 5
likelihood, 95
limitations, 8, 50, 69, 71, 77
linkage, 68
links, 22
liquefied natural gas, 1, 3, 36, 88
liquids, 9, 32
LNG, 1, 3, 6, 7, 9, 10, 16, 18, 20, 25, 31, 32, 36, 40, 45, 46, 47, 49, 50, 51, 52, 53, 54, 75, 77, 78, 81, 83, 88, 92, 99, 100, 101, 105
lobsters, 33
local authorities, 74
local government, 5, 6, 13, 15, 52
location, 15, 44, 48, 61, 66, 71, 73, 93, 94
location information, 44
long distance, 3
Los Angeles, 37, 102
losses, 8, 37
Louisiana, 1, 16, 99, 101
LPG, 1, 3, 7, 25, 31, 32, 46, 49, 50, 92, 99, 102
lubricants, 91

M

magnetic, iv
maintenance, 17
Malaysia, 18, 22, 43, 93
malicious, 25, 31
mammals, 34
management, 5, 6, 23, 48, 51, 53, 58, 64, 66, 67, 68, 87, 88, 89, 95, 96, 97, 101
mandates, 65
manpower, 52
manufacturing, 92
marine environment, 5, 71, 73
marine mammals, 34

maritime, 5, 10, 13, 15, 20, 21, 22, 25, 26, 27, 28, 29, 30, 31, 35, 39, 45, 58, 59, 65, 68, 83, 84, 87, 88, 89, 100, 101, 103, 104, 105, 106, 107, 108
Maritime Administration, 43, 88, 89, 99, 101
Maritime Transportation Security Act, 1, 4, 9, 26, 59
market, 5, 26, 34, 37, 38, 100
market prices, 38
markets, 22, 37
Maryland, 99
Massachusetts, 36, 46, 99, 102
measurement, 89
measures, vii, 5, 6, 8, 9, 10, 40, 41, 46, 50, 55, 74, 75, 79, 82, 85, 87, 88, 89, 96, 106
Mediterranean, 22, 31
methane, 92, 99
metropolitan area, 22
Mexico, 3, 18, 36, 99, 101
Middle East, 16, 22
migrant, 103
militant, 29, 93
military, 27, 29, 44, 59, 92, 104, 105
million barrels per day, 36
missions, 48, 51, 52, 54, 81, 103
mixing, 33
models, 37
money, 5
mortality, 33
MOU, 58
movement, 22, 36, 37, 44, 55

N

nation, vii, 3, 17, 21, 22, 23, 31, 35, 45, 50, 64, 73, 74
national, 9, 10, 22, 23, 34, 37, 54, 55, 56, 57, 58, 59, 63, 64, 67, 68, 78, 81, 83, 84, 89, 101, 106
National Incident Management System (NIMS), 57, 58
National Preparedness Goal, 63
National Research Council, 102

National Response Plan, 2, 9, 10, 56, 57, 68, 81, 84
National Response Plan (NRP), 56, 57
national security, 59, 68
National Strategy, 22, 58, 59, 101
natural, 1, 3, 4, 16, 18, 20, 36, 88, 92, 99, 100, 101, 106
natural disasters, 100, 106
natural gas, 1, 3, 4, 16, 18, 20, 36, 88, 92, 99, 101
Navy, 15, 17, 27, 31, 39, 42, 44, 87, 93, 103
Netherlands, 41
network, 34, 73
New England, 36
New Jersey, 68
New York, iii, iv, 68, 74
Niger, 93
Nigeria, 3, 18, 29, 93
nitrate, 49
nitrogen, 92
normal, 43, 49, 101
Northeast, 36
nuclear, 35
nuclear power, 35
nuclear power plant, 35

O

oat, 4, 93
observations, 100
oceans, 3
Offices of Congressional Relations and Public Affairs, 86
offshore, 4, 8, 16, 22, 27, 29, 31, 99, 104
offshore oil, 4, 27, 29, 31
oil, vii, 3, 4, 5, 6, 7, 9, 16, 17, 18, 20, 21, 25, 27, 28, 29, 30, 31, 32, 33, 34, 35, 36, 37, 42, 47, 49, 57, 58, 59, 61, 63, 66, 89, 91, 92, 93, 94, 99, 100, 101, 102, 106
Oil Pollution Act of 1990, 2, 5, 9, 17, 59, 69
oil production, 28
oil refining, 92

oil spill, 5, 9, 33, 34, 35, 37, 59, 66, 94
oils, 33, 91
Oman, 18, 21, 43, 44
operator, 52, 103
oral, 83
organization, 14, 41, 58, 71, 73, 97, 106
organizations, 5, 6, 9, 13, 14, 39, 59, 61, 71, 73, 87, 88, 104
oversight, 4, 5, 45

P

Pacific, 4, 22, 103, 107
Pacific Region, 103
Pakistan, 43
Panama, 22
partnership, 84
partnerships, 47, 53
passenger, 15, 61
penalties, 5
perception, 38, 46
performance, 10, 55, 64, 65, 74, 75, 79, 82, 85, 89, 97, 104
permit, 105, 108
Persian Gulf, 8, 17, 21, 27, 29, 31, 36, 93
petrochemical, 92
petroleum, 1, 3, 5, 6, 8, 16, 18, 20, 21, 25, 31, 32, 33, 34, 35, 36, 47, 48, 87, 88, 91, 92, 99, 101
Petroleum, 19, 20, 36, 102
petroleum products, 3, 8, 18, 20, 25, 31, 33, 34, 91, 99, 101
phone, 73
pilots, 22
pipelines, 36
piracy, 14, 43
planning, 5, 9, 10, 26, 52, 56, 57, 58, 59, 62, 63, 64, 67, 69, 78, 81, 84, 106
plants, 33
plastics, 91
platforms, 42, 104
play, 3, 9, 13, 47
police, 5, 9, 61, 89
policymakers, 23
political instability, 22

pollution, 4, 58
population, 4, 46, 48, 66, 100
ports, vii, 2, 4, 7, 8, 9, 10, 13, 14, 15, 16, 22, 26, 27, 29, 30, 31, 35, 36, 37, 39, 40, 41, 43, 45, 46, 47, 48, 50, 52, 53, 55, 63, 65, 66, 68, 69, 70, 71, 72, 73, 74, 77, 78, 81, 84, 87, 88, 89, 100, 101, 103, 104, 105, 106
posture, 8
power, 35
power plant, 35
premiums, 14, 43
preparedness, 58, 67, 106
pressure, 102
prevention, 5, 55, 73, 74
prices, 35, 37
Prince William Sound, 34
priorities, 10, 23, 54, 55, 57, 59, 65, 68, 74, 78, 82, 89, 97, 106
priority-setting, 75
pristine, 22
private, 3, 9, 13, 14, 53, 59, 68, 71, 81, 87, 88, 89
private sector, 3, 13, 14, 53, 68, 81, 88
probability, 106
probe, 4
producers, 37
production, 18, 28, 34, 92
program, 17, 41, 44, 74, 78, 106
progress reports, 6
projectiles, 29
propane, 92, 99
property, iv, 48, 63
protection, 44, 45, 48, 77
protocols, 27, 58, 59, 68
public, 2, 7, 25, 31, 32, 33, 34, 46, 57, 59, 61, 65, 66, 67, 68, 71, 78, 88, 89, 96
public health, 59, 68, 88
public safety, 7, 25, 31, 32, 33, 34, 57, 61, 65, 66, 67, 78, 88, 89, 96
Puerto Rico, 105

Q

Qatar, 18

R

radiation, 32
radio, 48, 73, 94
radiological, 37
rail, 37
random, 100
range, 6, 13, 29, 35, 39, 45, 48, 50, 52, 60, 67, 71, 73, 74, 91
rebel, 29
recovery, 59, 61, 63, 67, 68, 73, 74, 78, 84
refineries, 46
refining, 36, 92
reflection, 78
refrigeration, 102
regional, 20, 31, 37, 44, 59, 106
regular, 14, 38, 45, 47, 48
regulations, 6, 17, 42, 48, 65, 104, 107
Regulatory Commission, 4, 6, 51, 88, 99
regulatory framework, 14
relationships, 15, 89
reliability, 6, 89
research, 14
reserves, 36
resource allocation, 10, 81, 83
resources, 5, 9, 10, 23, 40, 45, 48, 52, 53, 54, 55, 58, 59, 63, 64, 67, 69, 70, 71, 74, 77, 78, 82, 83, 89, 95
response time, 58, 71
responsibilities, 13, 45, 46, 48, 53, 58, 61, 63, 64, 65, 78, 81, 83, 84, 104
revenue, 27, 29
Rhode Island, 33
rice, 34
risk, 5, 6, 8, 10, 23, 25, 26, 31, 48, 49, 50, 53, 55, 65, 74, 77, 78, 82, 83, 87, 89, 95, 96, 97, 101, 104
risk assessment, 49, 50, 96
risk management, 6, 23, 48, 51, 53, 87, 95, 101
risks, 23, 43, 47, 49, 50, 77, 83, 95, 96, 97, 104, 105
road map, 75
RP, 56, 57
Russia, 18

S

safety, 5, 7, 13, 16, 17, 23, 25, 31, 32, 33, 34, 47, 49, 57, 61, 65, 66, 67, 78, 88, 89, 96, 100, 104
sample, 6, 88, 100
sampling, 100
sanctuaries, 22
satellite, 36, 103
Saudi Arabia, 3, 18, 28, 31, 93
scalable, 104
school, 75
scores, 50
SEA, 103
Secretary of Homeland Security, 10, 23, 59, 68, 81, 82, 85, 97
security, 2, 3, 4, 5, 6, 8, 9, 10, 13, 14, 15, 16, 21, 23, 26, 29, 31, 35, 39, 40, 41, 42, 43, 45, 46, 47, 48, 49, 50, 51, 52, 53, 54, 55, 58, 59, 65, 68, 73, 74, 77, 78, 81, 83, 87, 88, 89, 95, 96, 100, 101, 103, 104, 105, 106
sediments, 34
selecting, 23, 97
Sensitive Security Information, 2, 100, 106, 107
sensors, 48
September 11, 4, 22, 23, 26, 30, 43, 45, 66, 72, 103, 106
series, 101
services, iv
severity, 95
sharing, 15, 52, 53, 69, 89
Shell, 93
shipping, 3, 14, 20, 21, 22, 29, 40, 43, 59, 87, 93, 100
shock, 31, 37
shock waves, 37
shores, 44, 103
short period, 25, 31, 35
shortage, 38
short-term, 34
signals, 73, 103
simulation, 64
Singapore, 22, 41, 43, 93
sites, 64
skills, 103
smoke, 32
smuggling, 25
soil, 4, 25, 26
solutions, 53
Somalia, 29, 43, 44
South America, 16
Southeast Asia, 31, 93
speed, 30, 71, 94
spills, 17, 25, 32, 33, 34, 56, 57, 59
spot market, 38
stability, 70, 107
stakeholders, vii, 6, 8, 9, 13, 15, 16, 35, 39, 45, 50, 52, 55, 58, 59, 60, 66, 68, 77, 78, 82, 85, 89, 104
standardization, 107
standards, 4, 6, 9, 14, 15, 17, 41, 49, 74, 77, 89
state control, 17
State Department, 42, 102
state oversight, 45
storage, 34, 36
Strait of Hormuz, 21, 35
strategic, 20, 36, 59, 95
Strategic Petroleum Reserve, 36
strategies, 23, 52, 58, 104
strikes, 14
substances, 5
suicide, 4, 7, 25, 27, 28, 29, 93, 94
sulfur, 91, 104
sulfur dioxide, 104
suppliers, 16, 18
supply, vii, 3, 4, 5, 6, 8, 14, 16, 18, 20, 21, 29, 31, 34, 35, 36, 37, 39, 77, 100, 102
supply chain, vii, 3, 4, 5, 6, 8, 16, 20, 29, 39, 77, 100
supply disruption, 8, 34, 36, 102
surplus, 53
surveillance, 26, 103, 104
suspects, 61
synchronization, 105, 108
synthesis, 95
systems, 17, 22, 48, 69, 73, 89, 107

T

tactics, 103
takeover, 30
tankers, vii, 3, 4, 6, 7, 8, 9, 11, 13, 16, 17, 18, 20, 21, 22, 23, 25, 26, 27, 29, 30, 32, 35, 36, 39, 42, 43, 44, 45, 46, 47, 51, 61, 63, 69, 78, 82, 85, 87, 88, 89, 99, 101, 102, 103, 104, 108
tanks, 16, 32
targets, 22, 26, 27, 50, 78, 101
task force, 44
telephone, 65
television, 48
terminals, 3, 4, 7, 22, 27, 36, 42, 88, 93, 99
territorial, 31
terrorism, 8, 9, 10, 14, 15, 27, 40, 41, 43, 48, 55, 56, 57, 58, 59, 61, 62, 63, 64, 65, 66, 67, 68, 72, 73, 74, 78, 81, 84, 87, 88, 89, 100, 104, 105, 106, 107
terrorist, 5, 6, 7, 9, 22, 23, 26, 27, 30, 31, 37, 45, 47, 50, 55, 56, 57, 58, 59, 61, 62, 63, 65, 66, 68, 72, 78, 87, 88, 89, 100, 101, 103, 104, 105, 106
terrorist attack, 5, 6, 7, 9, 22, 23, 26, 27, 30, 37, 45, 50, 55, 56, 57, 58, 59, 61, 62, 63, 65, 66, 68, 72, 78, 87, 88, 89, 100, 101, 103, 105, 106
terrorist groups, 23
terrorists, 4, 7, 25, 27, 28, 29, 30, 31, 42
testimony, 68
theft, 29, 102
third party, 40
threat, 7, 23, 25, 26, 29, 30, 32, 35, 49, 50, 82, 87, 95, 101
threatened, 8, 29, 35, 77
threats, vii, 6, 7, 10, 23, 25, 26, 30, 31, 35, 47, 58, 77, 85, 87, 95, 96, 108
time, 10, 25, 31, 33, 36, 44, 50, 55, 56, 58, 61, 65, 68, 71, 73, 74, 85, 104
toxic, 104
tracking, 44, 89
trade, 5, 27, 37, 59, 67, 68, 87, 102
trade diversion, 37
trade-off, 5

traffic, 34, 46, 49, 59, 77
trainees, 26
training, 26, 53, 55, 63, 64, 66, 67, 69, 71, 72, 74, 75, 89, 107
transfer, 16
transnational, 105
transport, 3, 4, 30, 34, 35
transportation, 2, 3, 5, 22, 27, 35, 37, 58, 59, 84, 101, 105
transportation security, 27, 35, 58, 59, 105
travel, 4, 8, 22, 32, 33, 43, 44
Trinidad and Tobago, 3, 18
trucks, 37
TSA, 4, 103

U

U.S. economy, 37
underwriters, 14
unemployment, 37
United Kingdom, 18, 43
United Nations, 100
United States, v, 2, 3, 4, 5, 6, 8, 9, 13, 14, 15, 16, 17, 18, 19, 20, 21, 22, 26, 36, 41, 42, 43, 44, 45, 55, 58, 77, 87, 88, 91, 99, 101
urban centers, 23

V

Valdez, 5, 33, 34, 35, 37, 102
vapor, 1, 32
variability, 66
vehicles, 28, 92
Venezuela, 3, 18
Very Large Crude Carriers, 16, 34, 101
vessels, 3, 4, 7, 8, 10, 14, 15, 17, 20, 22, 27, 30, 31, 39, 40, 41, 42, 43, 44, 45, 49, 50, 51, 55, 56, 59, 68
victims, 61
vinyl chloride, 49
Visa, 15, 42, 43, 103
visas, 15, 42, 102
vulnerability, 22, 23, 45, 50, 95, 96

Index 117

W

war, 14
water, 9, 15, 16, 22, 31, 33, 35, 56, 57, 61, 64, 73, 75, 107
waterways, 3, 22, 27, 35, 39, 43, 45, 59, 77, 103, 104, 106
weapons, 29
welfare, 8

wildlife, 32
winter, 36
workers, 7, 37, 93
workload, 9, 45, 48, 51, 78, 89

Y

Yemen, 4, 7, 28, 94
yield, 95